HISTORIC
NEWFOUNDLAND
AND LABRADOR

By The Late
L.E.F. English

**Prehistoric People of
Newfoundland and Labrador**

The Basque in Labrador
by James A. Tuck

The Beothuks
by Paul Carignan

The Vikings in Newfoundand

The Portuguese in Newfoundland Waters
by D.J. Wheeler

Published by
Department of Development and Tourism
Province of Newfoundland and Labrador
Honourable H.M. Barrett. M.H.A.
Minister

First Printing 1955
19th (Revised) Edition 1988

*For information or assistance
in vacation planning, contact:*
Department of Development
Tourism Branch
P. O. Box 2016
St. John's, Newfoundland
Canada
A1C 5R8

*Designed and Produced by
Ted Mills & Associates Ltd.*

Illustrations by Elaine Frampton

Contents

Introduction

The Newfoundland Department of Development is proud to include in its range of material describing the Province of Newfoundland, this booklet, which deals with the romantic history of Britain's Oldest Colony — Canada's Newest Province.

The information was gathered and collated by one of the foremost authorities on Newfoundland history and folklore, the late L.E.F. English, M.B.E. Mr. English relates Newfoundland's story in a popular style that makes for exciting reading, apart entirely from the educational worth of such a publication.

Because of the importance of archaeological discoveries made at Port au Choix and L'Anse-aux-Meadows since this booklet was originally published, supplementary articles on the aboriginal inhabitants of Newfoundland and Labrador and on the Viking voyages have been added to the current reprint. An additional section gives a brief account of the long history of the Portuguese in Newfoundland waters.

This is important reading, for, in a sense, the early history of Newfoundland is that of all North America. This great island is recognized as the cradle of European colonial settlement in North America; settlers were wrestling a living from the seas around Newfoundland shores when New York, Chicago, Toronto and Vancouver were not dreamed of even by the most optimistic empire builders. Squantum, an Indian who had learned the English language in Newfoundland, surprised the Pilgrim Fathers when they landed at Plymouth rock by welcoming them in their own tongue.

The booklet has been prepared with two-fold purpose in mind. It is hoped that the presentation of historical data in this fashion will give new impetus to those of our island who are interested in preserving that which reminds us of our great heritage. It is hoped, too, that this booklet will prove of great interest to the thousands of tourists who have planned, or will plan, a visit to Newfoundland.

The Lure
of Newfoundland

Come to Newfoundland! It is the cradle of European colonial settlement in North America. It is the region where the Viking adventurers landed in Anno Domino One Thousand and One and named the newly discovered country Markland or Land of Forest. It is the New Founde Isle of John Cabot who sailed westward from Bristol in 1497 and made his landfall at Cape Bonavista. It is the proud honour of ranking as the first of Britain's overseas colonies, for John Cabot set up the flag of England here and took possession in the name of his sovereign, King Henry VII. On the fifth of August, 1583, Sir Humphrey Gilbert reaffirmed this right of British ownership when he claimed the island in the name of Queen Elizabeth I, and on the King's Beach in the Harbour of St. John's, set up the first colonial government of Britain, overseas. Here, too, in more modern times, were wrought some of the greatest accomplishments of Science. In the year 1866, the "Great Eastern", wonder ship of her day, landed at Heart's Content the first successful Atlantic cable. At Cabot Tower on Signal Hill, St. John's, Guglielmo Marconi received the first wireless signals across the Atlantic on December 12th., 1901. From Lester's Field in St. John's the intrepid airmen Alcock and Brown took off for the first nonstop flight from America to Europe on June 14th., 1919. Coming down to still more recent date, it was in the placid harbor of Argentia that Roosevelt and Churchill drafted the terms of the Atlantic Charter.

Newfoundland is indeed rich in history. Its place names boast a dozen different languages, mute testimony of peoples who came and went and left on bay and island and headland records of their faiths and home memories. Here, War's red tide swept in all its fury when Britain and France fought for dominion in North America through many bitter campaigns of the seventeenth and eighteenth centuries.

Here on the wind swept slopes of Signal Hill was finally decided the last battle of the Seven Years War. Ruins of old forts with their ancient cannon may still be seen. At Placentia the former French capital, are ancient tombstones inscribed in the Basque language, the only relics of their kind in North America. In the west, the tourist may still listen to the

Acadian language that Evangeline and Gabriel spoke by the Minas Basin, as told by the poet Longfellow in his pathetic story of their sad romance.

Visit the fishing villages, the so called outports of the Province of Newfoundland. Listen to the quaint language of the folk, and hear the English speech, as it was pronounced in Devonshire in the time of Shakespeare. Or, linger awhile in the settlements where are located the descendants of Irish immigrants, and hear the rolling accent of Cork or the rich burr of a Kerry brogue. Ask for a thrilling ghost story or an intriguing tale of pirate treasure, and you have folk legends galore. Or it may be that you would be invited to hearken to fairy magic and watch the little fellows dance on the greensward in truly bewitching moonlight. Join in the merry throngs that laughingly tread the reels and quadrilles to the music of the village fiddler. Hear the folk songs of England and Ireland, songs that today are remembered only in the sequestered hamlets on the Newfoundland seashore. Revel in the supreme thrill of realizing that the welcome given the stranger comes from the heart of a delightful people who are remarkable above all else as the most hospitable folk in the whole world.

Take a sea trip down to Labrador, the great northern expanse of Newfoundland. The invigorating ozone from the sea is refreshing to the fevered brow of care and is Nature's best recipe for restoring colour to the pallid face of the invalid. Gaze enthralled on the rock ribbed bastions of Belle Isle or the two thousand foot sea wall of Cape Mugford. Marvel at the seaman's skill that guides the steamer through mazes of islands and channels and weaves a sinuous passage from Rigolet to the placid inland sea of Hamilton Inlet. You are in an Empire of the North, just now about to come into its own.

Newfoundland offers all these, and more! For the historian and the antiquarian there are trails of vanished races and international rivalries; for the artist there are scenic wonders of entrancing beauty; for the lover of outdoor sport there are unrivalled opportunities for trout, salmon and tuna fishing, and for wild duck, ptarmigan, caribou and moose hunting. The climate is temperate, cooled in summer by winds that sing up from the sea, and moderated in winter by these same winds that on the coast rarely permit zero weather.

We quote from the pen of Lt. Col. William Wood, a noted Canadian author and historian, the following picturesque tribute to Newfoundland and Labrador:

"Newfoundland is an island of the sea, if ever there was one. Nowhere else does the sea enter so intimately into the life of a people — calling, always calling them — loudly along a thousand miles of surf washed coastline, echoingly up a hundred resounding fiords that search out the very heart of the land, whisperingly through a thousand snug little lisping tickles, — but calling, always calling its sons away to the fishing grounds and sometimes to the seafaring ends of the earth.

"Labrador is a wild land, ruthless and bare and strong, that seems to have risen overnight from chaos, dripping wet . . . It is indeed very much as the Great Ice Era left it thousands and thousands of years ago. But even glacial times are modern compared with its real age. Its formation is older, far older than man; it is older than the original progenitors of all our fellow beings; millions of years ago. It is the very core of the great azoic Laurentians, the only land now left on the face of earth that actually stood by when Life itself was born."

7

Old St. John's

What hoary traditions entwine about the old town of St. John's caressed by the wild Atlantic surge! It's history, as far as can be ascertained from written records, goes back to the time of John Cabot, who, according to English seamen's tradition entered the harbour on the evening of St. John's Day in the year of our Lord 1497. From the very first years after Cabot's discovery, ships of Western Europe came to Newfoundland to fish, and St. John's was a rendezvous for them all. Captain John Rut of the British Navy described his visit there in 1527, and on board his ship, the "Mary of Guildford", he wrote the first letter from North America to Europe and sent it home to King Henry VIII by an English ship that was returning with a load of codfish. It was at the suggestion of the same Captain Rut that the King commanded a West Country merchant named Bute to form a colony in Newfoundland. Bute came out to St. John's in the following year and built the first permanent residence in the island. Thus the founding of the town can be said to date from the year 1528.

Jacques Cartier, the famous French explorer, visited St. John's many times. It was there that he met Sieur Roberval in the early summer of 1542* when the latter tried to compel the Breton captain to return with him up the St. Lawrence River. Cartier eluded his superior by slipping out of the harbour at night and sailing back to France. Sir Bernard Drake made St. John's his headquarters

*Dawson: "The St. Lawrence Basin," p. 202

in 1585, when he was sent out on a mission from the British Admiralty; he captured many Spanish and Portuguese ships and brought their crews home as prisoners. This was an attempt to cripple the Armada which three years later launched an invasion of England.

Sir Humphrey Gilbert landed on King's Beach on August 5th., 1583, and in the name of Queen Elizabeth he claimed the island as a British possession. Gilbert was drowned on the return voyage to England, but a full description of the expedition was recorded by Captain Hayes, who commanded the "Golden Hind". He described St. John's as a populous place much frequented by ships. Hayes wrote of the substantial houses of the merchants doing business at the port, and told of a favourite walk along a path leading to the west end of the harbour to a spot called "The Garden," where grew wild roses, strawberries and other fruits in abundance. The path trod by Gilbert and his officers was the well known Water Street of today, which can rightly claim the distinction of being the oldest street in North America. "The Garden" of Gilbert's day is now a pleasant downtown park.

Here in the harbour of St. John's the fishing ships of half a dozen nations selected their Admirals to keep law and order in those old days of Rut and Drake and Gilbert. The Admiral held office for a week, when another was selected to keep unruly spirits in check. Thus each weekend saw the Feast of the newly-chosen, and custom demanded that he should invite all seamen aboard his ship and wine and dine the multitude. We can picture the carousal as brown ale and mead of Merrie England mixed with wines of the sunny South, and toasts to

home were offered in rude mugs of baked clay held high in horny and unsteady hands while songs of diverse tongues made the welkin ring in boisterous chorus. Rule by Fishing Admiral was sanctioned by English law in 1633, when captain of the first ship to arrive in a harbour was to be admiral of such harbour for that season.

St. John's was several times attacked by enemy forces from both land and sea. A Dutch squadron under the famous De Ruyter took the town in 1665 and plundered it. A second attempt was made in 1673, but this time it was defended by Christopher Martin, an English merchant captain. Martin landed six cannons from his vessel, the "Elias Andrews", and constructed an earthen breastwork and battery near chain rock commanding the Narrows leading into the harbour. With only twenty-three men, the valiant Martin beat off an attack by three Dutch warships. Later in the same year, the gallant company defied the attempts of a pirate squadron to raid the town. After these attacks, forts were erected at both sides of the Narrows. In 1689, a large fort was completed, known as Fort William, it stood where the present Hotel Newfoundland looks over the city. A second fort, known as Fort George was situated at the east end of the harbour. It was connected by a subterranean passage with Fort William. On the south side of the Narrows there was a third fortification called the Castle.

The town was captured by French troops from Placentia in 1696, and again in 1708. The French burned the town on both occasions and destroyed the forts, carrying the guns to their stronghold at Placentia. After the second capture of St. John's, better and stronger fortifications were built by the English, and garrisons of British soldiers were maintained in anticipation of a renewal of enemy invasion. The town was captured for the last time in the summer of 1762, but it was quickly retaken by British troops despatched from Halifax under Colonel William Amherst. Fort Townshend was subsequently built on a commanding height above the centre of the town, and several strong forts were placed at the top of Signal Hill and at Fort Amherst on the south side of the Narrows. Garrisons were withdrawn from St. John's in 1871, and the fortifications were dismantled by orders of the British Government.

A visitor to St. John's today sees a thriving city that is rapidly spreading to the north and west.
Among the finest buildings may be included the Anglican Cathedral, which is said to be the best example of Gothic architecture in America, and the Roman Catholic Basilica which, at the time of its completion a century ago, was the largest church in the northern half of the New World. Government House, with its spacious grounds, and the Colonial Building with its massive columns of grey limestone are well worth a visit from the history lover.

The Newfoundland Museum is located on Duckworth Street and in the restored Murray Premises on the harbour apron. The main museum features exhibits spanning the prehistoric Maritime Archaic Indian Tradition; the native aboriginal groups within the Province including relics of the extinct Beothuk Indians who once roamed the forests and seacoast of the Central Nefoundland region. The Museum's displays recreate the exciting colonial history of the Province, depicting a colorful way of life wrestled from the land and the sea. The Murray Premises houses artifacts of the military, maritime and natural history of Newfoundland and Labrador.

In proximity to St. John's, are many quaint fishing villages. A half hour's drive by car takes the tourist to enchanting coastal scenery and through the old fashioned lanes lined with homes of the fisherfolk. And if one is minded to view more modern sights, there is the new campus of Memorial University, the Arts and Culture Centre and a variety of new schools, churches and commercial and residential developments.

Towns Of Conception Bay

A brief motor drive from St. John's takes the visitor to several picturesque and historic towns of Conception Bay. The bay itself was named by the Portuguese discoverer, Gaspar Corte-Real, who came in the year 1500 and claimed the island as part of Portugal's dominion under the famous "Linea Divisionis" which divided the New World between Portugal and Spain.

A first glimpse of the bay from the heights above the Topsail driveway shows Bell Island and Kelly's Island and beyond these the far outlines of the North Shore in blue distance. Kelly's Island received its name from a noted pirate who had a rendezvous there three centuries ago. In a lagoon on the east of the island may still be seen a large anchor imbedded in the beach where the bold Kelly careened his ships and refitted them for further piratical raids on transatlantic trade. Legend holds that somewhere on the Island lies the fabulous hoard hidden by the fierce sea rover of other days.

Holyrood is at the head of the bay. The scenery is delightful, and in the vicinity are several salmon and trout streams. Farther along the route are Harbour Main and Brigus, two of the oldest settlements in the province of Newfoundland. Harbour Main received its name from Saint Men of Britany who was a patron of fishermen from the port of St.

John Guy

Malo. Brigus is perhaps a form of Brick-house. One still gets the impression here of a typical English village with quaint old fashioned cottages and rugged towering elms.

Next we come to Cupids, the first official settlement in the island. Here in 1610, John Guy of Bristol, located his colony under charter from King James the First of England. Guy brought out a company of thirty-nine and built his plantation at the head of the small harbour then known as Cuper's Cove. The letters which Guy wrote home to the parent company have been preserved in Bristol, England, and they tell of the first winter spent in Newfoundland and give a description of the buildings erected under his personal supervision.

At the head of Bay de Grave, Guy had a sawmill and there too, he made experiments at farming in the New land. Owing to piratical raids and the opposition of West England fishermen the colony did not prosper. A granite monument reminds the visitor that here once was laid the foundation of English speaking America.

Further along the west side of Conception Bay the thriving towns of Bay Roberts and Spaniards Bay greet the eye of the stranger. The former received its name from fishermen of Jersey who came out from the Channel Islands in the sixteenth century. The latter is a reminder that at one time Spain did a remunerative trade in the fishing industry in Newfoundland waters, an industry that as far as Spanish fishermen were concerned ceased with the defeat of the Armada in 1588.

Next we come to the old town of Harbour Grace. Much of its former glamour has departed, but it is still rich in history and in pride of achievement. Its name is from the French, and it was called Harve de Grace possibly as early as 1505.

For a long time Harbour Grace was known as the metropolis of Conception Bay and was the second town in Newfoundland, ranking in trade and population next to St. John's. It was the terminus of the first railway around the Bay, there were many wealthy business houses, and there were flourishing seal and cod fisheries. The town was captured and looted by French troops in 1696. Part of John Guy's colony at Cupids had moved to Harbour Grace and to the neighbouring roadstead of Bristol's Hope. Fishing merchants from Jersey had been doing business there as early as 1560. The famous pirate captain, Peter Easton, had his headquarters at Harbour Grace about the year 1600, and his fort was located near the site of the stately Cathedral in the eastern part of the town. Harbour Grace was prominent in the first attempts of airmen to fly the transatlantic crossing, and boasted the only landing field in Newfoundland at that time.

Four miles north of Harbour Grace is Carbonear. The name of this town has puzzled students of Newfoundland nomenclature as to its correct derivation. Charbonniere, the French term for charcoal pot, is generally accepted as the origin. Some authorities have claimed that it is a corruption of Cape Carveiro, as the name appears in this form on some of the oldest maps of Newfoundland. It was a centre of the fishing trade away back in the sixteenth century. The town was taken and burnt by the French in their raids in 1696, but the inhabitants retired to an island in the mouth of the harbour and defied all attempts of the enemy to dislodge them. Some ancient cannons that were used to defend the town may still be seen. A legend that still lingers among Carbonear people concerns an Irish princess named Sheila Na Geira. Away back in the reign of Queen Elizabeth I of England the princess was captured in the English Channel by a sea rover named Gilbert Pike. He had captained a vessel belonging to Easton, but a quarrel ensued over some division of spoils and Pike went into piracy on his own. He was enamoured by the dark haired Irish beauty, and she in turn fell in love with the dashing and handsome corsair. She persuaded him to forsake his errant ways, and they came to Newfoundland and made their home at Carbonear. A child was born there, which tradition holds was the first white child to claim birth in Newfoundland. In the west end of the town may be seen a large tombstone in a private garden, and on it are engraved names of the Pike family. Beneath this stone are said to lie the ashes of Sheila Na Geira and her pirate lover.

Ferryland

*A*uthorities differ on the derivation of the name Ferryland. It has been written as Forillon, Foriland, and considered by some as a corruption of Veralum which was the ancient name of St. Alban's in England. It was first visited by French fishermen as early as 1504 and used by them as a base for summer fishery. It was these who called it Forillon, which meant "standing out or separated from the mainland" and thus aptly described the peninsula now known as the Downs.

The French abandoned their east coast resorts early in the sixteenth century and went each summer to the south coast where fishing began a month earlier. Englishmen then came and built temporary quarters at Ferryland, and so a century passed until Sir George Calvert, the first Lord Baltimore, applied in 1621 for a royal charter to colonize a portion of Newfoundland. In 1622 he received a grant of part of the southeastern peninsula, with quasi-royal jurisdiction. He named his province Avalon.

Captains Powell and Wynne were sent out to Ferryland as Baltimore's agents to supervise construction work. Wynne thus described the progress made up to late autumn of 1622; "The range of buildings was forty foot of length and fifteen foot of breadth, containing a hall, entry, cellar, four chambers, kitchen, staircases and passages. A face of defense was raised to the water sideward." After Christmas there were added a parlour fourteen feet long and twelve feet broad, a lodging chamber, a forge, salt works, a well sixteen feet deep, a brew house, a wharf, and a fortification "so that the whole may be made a pretty street." Land was cleared and in the spring wheat, barley, oats, beans, peas, radishes, lettuce, turnips, cabbage, carrots and kale were sown. Baltimore spent forty thousand pounds on his colony, but profits were slow of realization and he tardily began to suspect that all was not well. He came out with his family in 1627.* In his letters to King Charles I he complained of raids by French Men of War and requested protection by British ships. Lady Baltimore found the vigorous climate too severe for her frail health and in 1629 she and her son Cecil left Newfoundland for Virginia. Her husband then decided to abandon Ferryland and obtained a grant of land in Virginia, whither he and many of his colonists removed.

Calvert's province in Newfoundland had been named Avalon. Around this name centres the most beautiful legend in our island story. It carries us back to the beginning of the Christian Era, and to the occupation of Britain by Roman legions. It was Joseph of Arimethea who took the body of Christ from the cross, and it was the same Joseph of Arimethea who first preached the Gospel in Britain. At Glastonbury in Somerset, he built a church, and, in time, a great monastery was erected there. It was there the tomb of King Arthur was found in 1191. Glastonbury was surrounded by fens and was called the Isle of Avalon. Among the ruins of this hallowed spot, there blooms twice each year a hawthorn tree still known as the sacred thorn. Tradition tells us that Joseph carried with him to Britain a staff from the veritable tree whence came the crown of thorns that Christ carried at the Crucifixion. The disciple planted the staff at Avalon, where it lives and flowers at each May and Christmastide. Baltimore, who was a graduate of Oxford, was thoroughly versed in English legend. He envisioned an Avalon in the far West, where, like Joseph of old, he would build a shrine of faith amid the darkness of heathen lands. He brought missionaries with him who, like Arthur's knights were pledged:

"To reverence the king as if he were their conscience, and their conscience as their king.
To break the heathen and uphold the Christ."

We quote the following from Archbishop Howley's Ecclesiastical History of Newfoundland:

"Calvert seems to have been so thoroughly inbued with this idea of establishing Christianity in the New World, that it lends a tinge to each incident of his enterprise. Thus we find that he gave the

*Archbishop Howley "Ecclesiastical History" p. 104

name "The Ark of Avalon" to the principal ship, and that of "The Dove" to her pinnace. On a coin which he had stamped is seen a thorn with the motto "Spina Sanctus" (Sanctified by the thorn). It shows on the obverse side a harp of lyre, surrounded by a wreath of bay leaves and bearing the inscriptions, beneath the lyre "Orpheus" and above, the Greek legend "The air is the best" (Ariston men Aer). There is a mitre, crosier and cross, and a shield with a thorn and oak. On the margin are the words "Pro Patria et Avalonia".

Eight years after Baltimore vacated Ferryland, Sir David Kirke took over the property under charter from the Crown. Kirke was born in Dieppe, France, the son of a London Merchant and a French mother. Because of religious troubles he came to London and he and his brother were given a commission by King Charles I to outfit warships to prey on French commerce. Kirke made possible the colonization of Nova Scotia by Sir Alexander Macdonald, and captured eighteen French sail bound for Quebec. That town was forced to capitulate in the following year, 1629. Peace was proclaimed between England and France, and Kirke was ordered to restore the booty which he had taken. To recom-

pense him for losses thus sustained, he was given a grant of Newfoundland. He established his headquarters at Ferryland. Kirke, like Baltimore, was a staunch Loyalist and during the struggle between King and Parliament he offered Charles a refuge at Ferryland. He fitted out a fleet of ships manned with heavy guns to make an invasion of England in conjunction with Prince Rupert of the Rhine. The plan did not eventuate, and the victorious Parliament called Kirke home to England to answer the charge of rebel. As he had not actually taken part in the war, he was allowed to return to Newfoundland, but as a precaution Oliver Cromwell sent a British fleet to take every gun out of Ferryland. Kirke died there in 1655,* and was buried on the Downs. The place of his tomb is unknown to this day.

Nothing remains of the costly mansion in which Baltimore and Kirke once lived in vice regal splendour. The latter had repaired and improved the huge brick building and had added towers when it was proposed to house the King of England. The building was partly destroyed by the Dutch in 1673, when they sacked the town of Ferryland. Its proximity to the sea, and exposure to winter storms reduced the mansion to a heap of ruins. It was later used as a stone quarry by fishermen.

*Dawson: "The St. Lawrence Basin," p. 81

Other Old Colonies

Beyond Ferryland, in the electoral district of that name, are the fishing villages of Renews and Trepassey. These are the sites of two early colonies, the latter being that of Sir William Vaughan, the author of "The Golden Fleece", and the former, the location chosen by Falkland, Lord Deputy of Ireland. Both these abortive attempts at settlement antedated Baltimore's Avalon. Contrasted with the magnitude and expense of Calvert's pretentious undertaking, the more southern outlays did not involve the construction of stately mansions or impregnable forts. They were not backed by any considerable finance, and appeared doomed to failure from the beginning. Yet, at this distant date, it is certain that these have produced in their ultimate effects, a lasting impression on the distinctive character today known as the Newfoundlander. This is particularly true of the Falkland colony which brought to Newfoundland the first Irish settlers.

John Guy's grant of 1610 extended from Cape Bonavista to Cape St. Mary's. In 1616 the company of which Guy was the Newfoundland agent, sold part of its territory to Sir William Vaughan. He brought out a small party of colonists to the area near Trepassey, and these were mainly Welsh people. Vaughan himself was an idealist, and spent his time in writing books. The settlers were not fishermen or seamen of the type from Devon. They appear to have been lacking in necessary industry and initiative, and were content to occupy huts erected for summer fishermen. Vaughan subsequently sold part of his land to Lord Baltimore in order to avoid insolvency. The colonists were left to shift for themselves. French fisher-

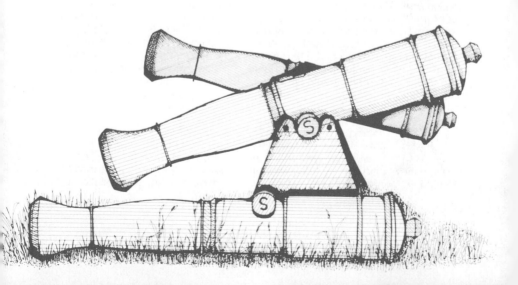

men occupied the best sites at Trepassey and moved to other places nearer to St. John's, or hired as servants to Merchant Adventurers whose fishing ships came each summer to the harbours of the Southern Shore.

In Prowse's History of Newfoundland one can read the prospectus of Lord Falkland's colonial scheme. In it are mentioned a South Falkland and a North Falkland. The latter was located at Trinity in the bay of that name, and the former embraced the harbours of Renews and Fermeuse. Bands of colonists from Ireland, speaking the Celtic language, were brought to Newfoundland in 1619, but as in the case of Vaughan the plan lacked the necessary financial backing and the Irish were not fishermen. However, they lived on through adverse circumstances and though hounded out of their original holdings they trekked southward from Renews into St. Mary's Bay where for two centuries they fished and farmed and in their isolation held on to their parent speech. Those from the Trinity area went northward to Bird Island Cove, now renamed Elliston, and into Bonavista By and as far as Fogo Island. At Tilting on this island is one of the oldest cemeteries in Newfoundland. Today the coast from St. John's to the head of Placentia Bay is inhabited by descendants of the Irish people who were first brought to Newfoundland by Lord Falkland. That stream of immigration continued steadily until the middle of the nineteenth century.

A motor drive through the fishing villages from St. John's to Trepassey takes the visitor through that portion of the Avalon Peninsula most replete with historic associations. First there is Bay Bulls, its name derived from either Baie de Bois or Baie Boules. It is one of the oldest settlements of the province, harking back to the days of Welsh and Irish Colonies. It was captured by the French several times and burnt, the last occasion in 1796. At the entrance to the parish church may be seen gateposts made from ancient cannon.

Some twelve miles beyond Ferryland lies Renews. No place in Newfoundland has had its name suffer a greater variety of change. On the earliest Portuguese maps it is called Rognaza, a title probably given by seamen of that nation because of the great number of boulders tht appear above water in the harbour at low tide. It is called Rougenoust in an old French document in the National Library in Paris. This script was discovered by the historian Henry Harisse and reads: "Let a note be made of the marks of my boats and barks which I leave in Terre Neuve in the harbour of John Denys called Rougenoust." The name subsequently was changed to Renowse, and later to Renewse and Renews. Apparently the French had used the harbour, as a fishing station as early as 1506,* for that is the date of the script mentioned above. Remains of old forts may still be seen near the harbour entrance. Two or three old guns lie half buried beneath an earthen mound, and at a higher point there is a larger cannon in an excellent state of preservation.

Bay Bulls, Aquafort, and Fermeuse are good harbours, capable of affording shelter to fishing schooners and fleets of warships. The scenery along the Southern Shore is delightful, and this is true in particular of the La Manche Lakes, Tors Cove and Cape Broyle. There are good salmon rivers and excellent barrens for willow grouse, locally called partridge.

Placentia

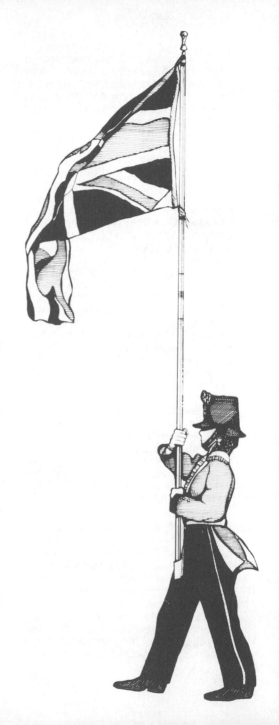

Verily, at Placentia you walk above the dust of Empire. The name itself carries you back to those far off times when Caesar's legions rested below the foothills of the Pyrenees and named their camping ground Placentia, a level disc within a womb of hills. Perhaps the Basques saw a physical resemblance here in the New Land to that spot in their own beloved country, and so they gave the name Placentia to this haven of level beach and harbour amid environing fir clad heights.

The Basques were among the first European fishermen to visit North America after its discovery by Cabot. Some historians claim that ships of the Basques actually had found the Grand Banks and the Isle of Codfish before the voyages of Cabot or Colombus. Recent marine archaeological evidence at Red Bay, Labrador lends evidence to the argument that the Basques were the first to penetrate the Strait of Belle Isle, where they found an abundance of whales, walruses and seals. They had fishing stations at Trepassey, St. Mary's, Placentia and Miquelon, which are all named from towns in their homeland. The chronicler Hakluyt relates that in

1592 an English captain named George Drake visited Placentia and found there sixty Basque ships. John Guy in his letters of 1611 tells how he intended to make a voyage to Placentia, a place of considerable trade.

The French followed the Basques to the south coast of Newfoundland and learned from them the best locations for the codfishery. Then in 1662 France decided to extend her western empire to include Newfoundland. as this island commanded the entrance to the St. Lawrence Gulf. They built strong forts at Placentia and maintained there garrisons of soldiers and several ships of war. When, towards the end of the seventeenth century, war broke out between England and France mainly over dominion in the western world, it was from Placentia that French forces overran the Avalon Peninsula and destroyed English settlements. In their turn British naval forces attempted to capture the French stronghold, but found the defences too strong to be taken by force. The Treaty of Utrecht in 1713 put an end to French occupation of Placentia, and by the terms of peace France evacuated Newfoundland and was given permission to fish on the northern coast. French nationals, thus expelled from Placentia, St. Pierre, and other south coast points, went to St. Mary's Bay on Cape Breton Island where they founded the great fortress of Louisburg.

*I*n the Museum at St. John's are plans of the French forts at Placentia as well as the locations of French fishing premise and the church and monastery. The main fort, known as Fort Louis, was on the Jersey side and commanded the entrance to the harbour. Here also were the residence of the commandant and officers' quarters. On the height known as Castle Hill, now a National Historic Site, was a stone redoubt which had several heavy cannons, and on a hill above Fort Louis was a smaller watch tower called the Gallardin. The Church of the Franciscans was near where the present Anglican chapel now stands, and where may still be seen ancient tombstones inscribed in the Basque language. One of these is in a good state of preservation and the inscription has been translated as "Here lies, having died on May 1st., 1676, John de Sale Cesana. Son of the House of Sweetest Odour". Another larger stone is of the table or altar type, and was erected to the memory of Suigarachipi, a Basque captain who had a distinguished career in the French navy. He died of wounds received in action against the British Fleet at Placentia.

When the English took over the forts at Placentia in 1713, they sent an army engineer to report on the condition of the defenses there. Fort Louis was found in a state of deterioration, and it was recommended that a new stronghold be built on what is now known as the Town Side. Accordingly, a more modern bastion of defense was constructed at the point of beach near the entrance to the Main Gut, and was called Fort Frederick. The fort on Castle Hill was repaired, and an additional battery was placed on the opposite side of the Roads about halfway to Point Verde. These various fortifications were maintained until some years after the peace which ended the Wars of Napoleon.

Nothing now remains of Basque and French occupation except the few mouldering tombstones to which we have already referred and the reconstructions of the fortifications on Castle Hill where visitors return again to the glory of France's former foothold in Newfoundland. Some old cannons have survived the passage of years, and have been placed in the neglected churchyard where the great altar slab of Suigarachipi lies broken in twain. His sleep beneath the beach is as sound as it might be in a cyrpress grove on the slopes of his native Pyrenees. One still reads on the gravestone the words "Cy Gis Joannes de Suigarachipi, Dit Croisic, Captaine de Fregate du Roi, Envieux, 1694. Pour L'Honneur de mon Prince J'Allais en suivant sa Carriere ,attaquer les ennemis . . . . ."

The proximity of the great naval base at Argentia has tended to modernize the old town of Placentia where many of the personnel from Fort McAndrew have taken up residence. The fishing fleets that formerly sailed each spring to the ledges off Cape St. Mary's and to the Grand Banks have disappeared from the harbour, and the long level beach no more holds the summer harvest of fish drying in the sun. The tides swirl up the town gut and into the copious arms that wind among the everlasting hills. The glory that once was the boast of the Ancient Capital lives only in names such as Brulé and Crèvecoeur. Old fishermen still tell of ghostly galleons that enter the roads in the darkness of night and of pinnaces that glide noiselessly under the shadows of Castle Hill and sweep and vanish beneath the gloom of Mount Pleasant.

Towns Of
The North

He who follows history's trails in Newfoundland need not confine his interest to the Avalon Peninsula. Northward along the rockbound shores there are places and names that allure the story lover and the writer of legendary lore. There are Trinity, Catalina, Bonavista, Fogo, Twillingate and St. Anthony, all with uncommon background of historical tradition.

We shall begin with the old town of Trinity, clinging to the base of Ryder's Hill and sheltered in one of the finest harbours in the world. Here in the year 1615 Sir Richard Whitbourne set up the first Court of Justice in North America. He was under orders from the British Admiralty to suppress crimes among the fishermen of European ships that came in hundreds to Newfoundland waters each summer. For several years Sir Richard carried on a successful business at Trinity and made notes for a book on Newfoundland which he subsequently published in England. A copy of Whitbourne's book was by Royal Command distributed to every parish in the kingdom.

Next in turn is Catalina, the harbour of St. Catherine, visited by Jacques Cartier in 1534. In his Relation Originals, the Breton captain vividly described his ten days stay at this port, where he was delayed by field ice. He spent the time profitably in outfitting his small boats for careful navigation when he reached unknown regions within the Gulf of St. Lawrence. From Catalina he sailed to the Funk Islands to obtain food supplies

from immense flocks of the Great Auk, and thence set his course for Belle Isle Strait. The harbour of Catalina today is perhaps better known by the great project and premises of the Fishermen's Union situated in the western arm. The tomb of its founder Sir William Coaker may be seen near the spacious hall and in proximity to his former home where this remarkable man of genius dominated the politics of the North.

Four miles north of Cape Bonavista lies the town of that name. The cape is the landfall of John Cabot, and was designated as such on Mason's map of 1620. Mason undoubtedly knew this as a tradition among English fishermen, or he may have copied from an older chart. Bonavista is one of the oldest settlements in Newfoundland, and its founding goes back to the days of the first Fishing Admirals when those bluff traders chose the best harbours and drove the resident fishermen into more remote and less sheltered coves. Bonavista was able to muster three hundred men during the French invasion of 1696 and resisted an attempt of the enemy ships to capture the settlement. In recent years an extensive breakwater has been constructed and the harbour dredged to permit passage to large schooners and coastal steamers. Modern fish plants and long line trawlers ensure prosperity to a large fishing population who gather a prolific harvest of the sea from the rich grounds off the cape.

Fogo town is on the north of Fogo Island. On the earliest maps the latter is spelled Fuego, and it is thus on the Ribeiro map of 1529. The name may have been given from some fancied resemblance to an island in the Cape Verde group, or perhaps the presence of Indian campfires inspired the visiting navigators to so name the island. The town is the oldest settlement north of Bonavista Bay, and dates back to 1680. On the east of the island is the village of Tilting to which we have previously referred. The name is a changed form of Tilt Town, and undoubtedly the later was so called from the primitive log huts of early Irish settlers. Near Tilting is Sandy Cove which was a favourite resort of the Beothuks in their annual migration to the coast. Tradition holds that a rock with red stains is the spot where a fisherman was murdered by the natives.

Twillingate has been called the capital of the north. It was founded about the same time as Fogo, and has been a centre of trade for Labrador and shore fisheries for two centuries. The name is derived from the French family surname Toulinquet, and was given by early fishermen from the land of the Fleur-de-Lys. It was the birthplace of the famous operatic singer Miss Toulinquet Stirling. At Twillingate there is a fine modern hospital which serves the needs of the people of Notre Dame Bay. Both Twillingate and Fogo were used as business centres by English firms who carried on a thriving trade in these northern towns two centuries ago. Besides the fishing industries, there was a lucrative barter in seals and furs, and in the lumber which could be obtained easily in the teeming forest areas of Gander and Exploits.

On the northern tip of the Great Northern Peninsula lies the town of St. Anthony, made famous by the work of that indefatigable friend of man, Dr. Wilfred Grenfell. His work is too well known to need any lengthy tribute.

The West Coast

The West Coast of Newfoundland from Port aux Basques to Cape Norman has a somewhat different historical background from that of the eastern parts of the province. Its settlement is more recent, its racial origins are more varied, and its economy has had a pattern of development all its own. A No Man's Land for two centuries, then for two more a disputed territory outside the pale of the law, it has been indeed the "sport of historic misfortune" of the most pronounced type.

In the month of June, 1534, Jacques Cartier of St. Malo explored the west coast of Terre Neuve. The story told in the plain language of the sailor has a fascinating appeal. He had gone up the west side of Belle Isle Strait as far as Brest, and then returned to the Newfoundland shore. First they saw what appeared to be two islands, but which were two lofty summits of the Long Range Mountains in the rear of Point Riche. During the following day they coasted southward with a light favouring wind. The mountains rose high and formidable in the background, and between them and the shore was a belt of woodland. Cartier named one lofty summit La Granche, because of its resemblance to a farmhouse. The two ships anchored for the night at Cap Pointu, now named Cow Head. A storm came on, and the cautious mariner ordered his vessels "hove to" in the Gulf. Two days later they were abreast of the Bay of Islands. Thence they explored Port-au-Port Bay, and while there found

codfish in abundance. Cartier described the isthmus now known as the Gravels, and the long spit of land to the west he named Cap Delatte. Again stormy weather forced the ships to head into open water, and after three days they sighted Cape Anguille which was named Cap St. Jean. From that point the vessels went westward as far as Gaspe, and returned to France by way of Belle Isle Strait. In the following year Cartier explored the St. Lawrence as far as Hochelaga, now Montreal. He wintered at Quebec and returned home by way of Cabot Strait, and was thus the first to circumnavigate the island.

The Treaty of Versailles in 1783 gave France the right to fish on the West Coast of Newfoundland. That nation claimed it was an exclusive right; Britain maintained it was concurrent. And so they wrangled and met in convention and procrastinated and the island of Newfoundland suffered in consequence. It was not until 1904 that the matter was finally settled when the French relinquished their claims in exchange for a strip of territory in West Africa. The electoral districts of St. George's and St. Barbe were first represented in the Newfoundland legislature in 1882, and customs officers had been appointed five years previously. The project of a railway across the island with a terminus at St. George's was banned by the British Government as late as 1890 on the ground that such terminus would be on what France regarded as her national soil.

While the racial origins of the East Coast are mainly four, the West of Newfoundland has eight distinct types. These are pure French stock, Acadian, Micmac, English, Channel Islanders, Irish, Scottish and Nova Scotian and French fishermen who deserted from ships of Basque and Biscayan ports. The French had fishing stations on the west of the Petit Nord Peninsula in the latter years of the seventeenth century. Acadians from the Minas Basin of Nova Scotia after the expulsion of 1755 came to Louisburg, and when that fortress fell in 1758 a wandering remnant crossed to Newfoundland and sought peace in the isolated coves of Bay St. George and the Port-au-Port Peninsula. Their descendants still speak a provincial Parisian dialect. Micmacs from Nova Scotia had been in the habit of crossing over to Newfoundland each autumn to hunt for furs, from about 1650 onward. They were on friendly terms with the Acadian French, and when the latter settled on the West Coast the Indians also took up permanent residence. The first English and Jersey traders came about 1770, and settled at St. George's and Bay of Islands. The Irish came west shortly after, and found employment with the merchant traders; lastly, Scottish farmers from Nova Scotia crossed over to Newfoundland about a century ago and began to make homes in the picturesque Codroy Valley.

The West Coast has many attractions for the tourist. It has the finest salmon streams in the province. Its scenery is the best of which Newfoundland can boast, and this is particularly true of the Codroy region, of Bay of Islands with its unrivalled Humber Valley, and Bonne Bay with its encircling mountains.

The heart of the economy of the West Coast lies at Corner Brook where is located one of the largest integrated pulp and paper mills in the world. Around this industrial centre has grown up a prosperous city that bids fair to vie in commercial importance with the position that the capital city of St. John's holds in the East.

Newfoundland Folklore

Folk Lore has been defined as race experience crystallized into story, song or saying. A visitor to Newfoundland is amused and charmed by the quaint speech of the fisherfolk and by the originality and picturesque form of their homemade phrases. The St. John's accent has a pronounced Irish quality, and the same may be said of the districts of Harbour Main, Ferryland and Placentia. In the north of the Island one hears an altogether different pronunciation, and listens to a Dorset or Devon dialect of three centuries ago with words and idioms long lost in England. More interesting than this variety of accent are the homely figures of speech that have their origin in environment through four centuries of settlement. These idioms have an unusual type of literary value because of their simplicity and their redolence of the things of Newfoundland life.

In the following pages we present a selection of Newfoundland folk lore which is classified under various headings. First we give a vocabulary of unusual words with their meanings. This is not by any means a full list, but has been culled from a collection gathered from every part of the province. Meanings and origins are given wherever possible; it is not always certain where a word originated, and its present spelling is obviously phonetic.

Next we give an interesting list of Newfoundland sayings. Some of these were brought out from England and Ireland by the early settlers. Others are of the type coined in this province, and are

moulded from contacts with nature through generations of hardy toilers of the sea. These are the most valuable portion of the island's folk lore, and are indeed the very essence of race experience. These sayings are of two kinds, one taking the form of a mere peculiar expression, and the second being a homely simile or metaphor terse and picturesque.

Lastly we give a heterogeneous group of legends of multiple classifications, such as weather lore, folk medicines, omens of good or bad luck, superstitions, and quaint customs. Our sources are many, and have been derived from a lengthy study of the island's traditions. For our description of Christmas customs we owe much to the late Rev. A. C. Waghorne, the author of "The Flora of Newfoundland". We have also received invaluable aid from the writings of the late P. K. Devine, H.W. LeMessurier, and W. A. Munn.

Words and Their Meanings

amphered;
infected, purulent

angishore:
a weak, miserable person

anighst;
near

aninst;
beside

arn;
any

atirt;
athwart

balderdash;
nonsense

bavin;
wood shavings to light fires

ballyrag;
to abuse

bannock;
a round cake of bread

ballycater;
ice formed by spray on the shore

bannikin;
a small tin cup

bawn;
a beach used to dry fish

barrisway;
a lagoon at a rivermouth; barachoix

bass;
to throw small stones

bedlamer;
a seal one yer old; bete de la mer

binicky;
ill-tempered

biver;
to shiver with cold

blather;
nonsensical talk

blear;
an ignorant person

bogie;
a small stove

bostoon;
to complain loudly

bonnif;
a young pig

brieze;
to press down firmly

breach;
schools of fish on the surface

brack;
a crack in a dish or furniture

brishney;
dry twigs gathered for fuel

brewis;
hard biscuit boiled, and pork fat

bultow;
a line with hooks, a trawl

calabogus;
rum, molasses and spruce beer

cant;
to lean to one side

chucklehead;
a stupid person

chinch;
to stow tightly

clink;
to beat another with the fists

clamper;
ice detached from berg of floe

clout;
to hit an opponent hard

clum;
to grapple with an adversary

clobber;
an untidy state of things

covel;
a covered water barrel

cotched;
caught

crannicks;
dried roots of trees

crossackle;
to vex by contrary argument

crubeens;
pickled pigs' feet

cuddy;
a covered space in the bow of a boat

daddle;
the hind paw of a seal

dill;
a cavity in a boat from which water is bailed

doter;
an old seal

douse;
to give a quick blow

drung;
a narrow, rocky lane

drook;
a valley with steep wooded slopes

dresser;
an old fashioned kitchen cupboard

drubbin;
oil and tallow to preserve boots

duckish;
the time between sunset and dark

duff;
pudding of flour, fat pork and molasses

dulse;
a kind of seaweed

dudeen;
a pipe

dwoi;
a short snow shower

faddle;
a bundle of firewood; fardel

faggot;
a pile of half-dried fish

fipper;
a seal's forepaw; flipper

flankers;
sparks from a chimney

flinders;
small pieces

fousty;
mouldy, with a bad odour

frore;
frozen

frape;
a rope with blocks to moor a boat

fudge;
to manage daily chores alone

funk;
smoke or vapour of evil odour

gansey;
a woollen sweater; from Guernsey

gamogue;
a silly trick

gandy;
a pancake

glutch;
to swallow with difficulty

glauvaun;
to complain about trifles

gommil;
a moron, a half fool

gruel;
oatmeal porridge

grumpus;
the whale

gulvin;
the stomach of a codfish

gurry;
blood and slime from fish

guff;
impertinence

gilderoy;
a proud person

gowdy;
awkward

gumbeens;
cubes of chewing tobacco

helf;
the handle of an axe, haft

heft;
to weigh in the hand

huffed;
vexed

hummock;
a small hill

jackeen;
a rascally boy

jinker;
one who brings bad luck

jut;
to hit the elbow of another

kingcorn;
the Adam's apple of the throat

klick;
the stiffening at the back of a shoe

lashins;
plenty

lob;
not of much value

lolly;
soft ice beginning to form in harbour

longers;
rails for a fence

lourd;
dark, gloomy

lops;
small breaking seas

manus;
to mutiny aboard ship

mauzy;
misty

mundle;
a wooden baton used to stir soup

mush;
porridge

munch;
to grind with the teeth; from "manger"

narn;
none

nish;
tender, easily injured

omadhaun;
a foolish person

oonshick;
a person of low intelligence

peeze;
to leak in small bubbles

pishogue;
a story generally discredited

plaumaush;
soft talk, flattery

planchen;
the floor; from "plancher"

prise;
a lever

pritchet;
a prop under the shaft of a cart

prog;
food

puddock;
the stomach

quot;
to crouch; squat

quid;
a chew of tobacco; the cud

ral;
a disorderly fellow

rawny;
very thin, bony

rames;
a skeleton

rompse;
to wrestle

sadogue;
a fat, easy going person

scrammed;
numb with cold

scrawb;
to tear with the nails

scrimshank;
hesitation to avoid an issue

scut;
a dirty, mean person

shaugraun;
a vagabond state

sharoused;
nonplussed

scruff;
the back of the neck

sish;
ice broken into particles by surf

slob;
ice newly frozen

slinge;
to stay away from school or work

shooneen;
a coward

shule;
to move away backwards

smidge;
a stain

sloo;
to get out of the way

slieveen;
a deceitful person

suent;
smooth, graceful

snarbuckle;
a hard knot; burnt to a cinder

strouters;
posts at the end of a fishing stage

squabby;
soft as jelly

squish;
the sound of waters exuding from boots

spile;
a peg for a hole in a cask

sugawn;
a rope made of twisted hay

swatch;
to shoot seals in pools amid icefloes

swig;
to drink from a bottle

switchel;
cold tea

tacker;
waxed hemp for sewing boots

tant;
tall and slender, as trees and spars

talqual;
the good with the bad; talis qualis

tantem;
side by side

teeveen;
a patch on a boot

titivate;
to adorn exceedingly fine

tole;
to entice with bait

trapse;
to walk around unnecessarily

trunnel;
a wooden peg in a plank; trenail

truck;
payment for fish by merchandise

tuckamore;
a low clump of trees

twig;
to catch the meaning

twack;
to examine goods and buy nothing

vang;
fried salt pork

vamp;
the sole of a stocking; to walk

vandue;
a sale by auction; Vendu

wattle;
a small slim fir

weasand;
the throat

witlow;
inflammation around a fingernail

whiting;
a tree from which the rind has been removed

water horse;
salt fish just washed from a vat

wop;
the wasp. A blow from a blunt weapon

yarkin;
lines to fasten a net to a head rope

yean;
giving birth to young by sheep

yarry;
rising early; alert

yaffle;
an armful of dried fish

yer;
here

yoi;
in this place

yerrin;
a reef point; earing

yuck;
to vomit

yap;
to retort angrily

Newfoundland Sayings

As fine a man as ever broke a cake of the world's bread.

All mops and brooms.
This refers to an untidy condition of the hair.

An honest man when there are no anchors around.
Ironical tribute.

A fisherman is one rogue, a merchant is many.

A warm smoke is better than a cold fog.

A single line may have two hooks.
A dual purpose.

An Irish youngster for the bow oar.
He gets the spray over him.

A gunshot away.
A short distance, about fifty yards.

A noggin to scrape.
A very difficult task.

An hour by sun.
An hour before sunset.

Come day, go day, God send Sunday.
Applied to a lazy person.

Cape St. Mary's pays for all.
This locality has a prolific fishery.

Done it brown.
Overdid the thing – the allusion is to burnt bread.

Don't cut tails.
Don't be too particular. Fish tails were cut as a mark.

Douse the killock.
Throw the grapnel overboard.

Empty vessels loom biggest.

Fair weather to you and snow to your heels.
Good luck on your way.

Far off cows wear long horns.

Fish in summer and fun in winter.
Everything in its place.

Give her the long main sheet.
To go afar with no intention to return.

Go to law with the devil and hold court in hell.
The odds are all against you.

Good morrow to you.
You are mistaken.

Jack is as good as his master.
The hired man is paid off when the end of the fishing season arrives, and is no longer a servant.

In a hobble about it.
Not worrying about the matter.

If you lose your grapnel, you'll find it in the fall.
You will find it on your account at the merchant's store.

In a leaky punt with a broken oar, 'tis always best to hug the shore.

I'll go bail for that.
I will vouch for the truth of it.

Let no man steal your lines.
Beware of competition.

Long may your big jib draw.
A good wish for the future.

May snow is good for sore eyes.
An old legend; many say it is true.

Nofty was forty when he lost the pork.
Never be sure of anything; the man Nofty held the best trump but allowed an opponent to reach game.

Out dogs and in dieters.
Prepare for the summer fishery.

Praise the weather, when you're ashore.

Pigs may fly, but they are very unlikely birds.
Hope in vain.

Skin the old cow.
When cold March weather persists far into April the old cow dies of hunger.

Solomon Gosse's birthday.
This was Thursday when the usual was pork and cabbage and pudding, a favourite meal in Newfoundland.

The devil to pay and no pitch hot.
Unprepared for emergency. To "pay a boat" meant to put hot pitch over a seam between the planks.

There's favour in hell, if you bring your splits.
Said of currying favour through underhand methods.

Tom Long's account.
To pay what you owe and have nothing left.

'Tis not every day that Morris kills a cow.
Favourable opportunity comes but seldom.

The old dog for a hard road.
Experience easily overcomes difficulty.

White horses on the bay.
On a stormy day waves break into foam. The allusion to white horses is apparently a reference to an Irish tradition of a chieftain named O'Donahue who was drowned in a lake in Killarney on his wedding morn, and could afterwards be seen in a storm riding a white horse and preceded by maidens strewing flowers.

Wait a fair wind, and you'll get one.
Await opportunity.

When the snipe bawls, the lobster crawls.
After sunset.

You can't tell the mind of a squid.
This refers to an unreliable person. A squid can move backwards or forward.

You can get only one shot at a shell bird.
A shrewd person can be duped but once.

You are robbing Peter to pay Paul.
Needless change of useful things.

You'll do it in the long run.
Eventually you will succeed.

You are taking a rise out of me.
Your flattery is only for the purpose of making others laugh at me.

You are as deep as the grave.
Your real feelings are not easily judged from your appearance.

You are making a nice kettle of fish.
Making a mess of affairs.

You are moidering my brains.
Your noise is very distrubing.

Your tawts are too far aft.
The word "thwart", meaning a cross seat in a boat, is commonly pronounced "tawt" by Newfoundland fishermen. The expression means you are very wrong in your opinion.

You are too big for your boots.
You are assuming too much authority.

You can cut a notch in the beam.
Said when someone does the unusual.

You are like a fish out of water.
Not at home in your environment.

The older the crab, the tougher his claws.
It is not easy to fool a sophisticated person.

Figures Of Speech

Busy as a nailer

Black as soot

Big as Munn

Bold as brass

Brown as a berry

Cross as the cats

Crazy as a loo

Cute as a rat

Dark as pitch

Deaf as a haddock

Dirty as duck's puddle

Dry as a bone

Far as ever a puffin flew

Foolish as a caplin

Flat as a pancake

Hard as the hob of hell

Hard as the knockers of Newgate

Hungry as a hound

Ignorant as a pig

Like a northerly squall

Like a singed cat

Like a cat on hot rocks

Like a birch broom in the fits

Lazy as the dogs

Leaky as a basket

Lonesome as a gull on a rock

Mute as a mouse

Old as Buckley's goat

Proud as Guilderoy

Rotten as dirt

Rough as a dogfish's back

Round as the bung of a cask

Round as a barrel

Soft as mummy

Slow as cold molasses

Saucy as a crackie

Sore as a boil

Stiff as a poker

Solid as a rock

Smooth as a mill pond

Smooth as oil

Soggy as lead

Stunned as an owl

Smart as a bee

Straight as a ramrod

Sound as a bell

Smoky as a Labrador tilt

Thick as tar

Thin as an eggshell

Wet as dung

White as the driven snow

Wild as a deer

Wide as the devil's boots

Yellow as beaten gold

Weather Lore

Here again we find the result of race experience. The Newfoundland fisherman has to pursue his vocation in wind and sea, and generations of wisdom in forecasting storms have been handed down to him through the centuries. He has to foretell from nature just when favourable opportunity will present itself so that ventures to fishing ledges far from shore may be made with impunity. Also he has to predict rain so that fish may be spread when long periods of sunshine are practically certain. He knows the winds and ocean currents that offer the best conditions for a good catch, and he is familiar in his own way with the humidity of the atmosphere that is an adverse factor in the drying process. Below we give some of the more common signs of good and bad weather as long observed and religiously depended upon.

A red dawn is a sign of rain and storm.

A red sunset is a sign of fine weather.

Brilliant Northern Lights foretell a fine day and then a storm.

Hoar frost in autumn is a sign of south wind and rain.

When gulls fly high, stormy weather may be expected.

When goats come home from the hills, expect rain soon.

When distant hills appear near, rainy weather is coming.

Rote from the shore on a calm night indicates wind from that direction the following day.

When wild animals take on thick coats of fur in autumn, it is a sign of a severe winter.

After the sun crosses the line in September, watch the wind and weather for the following days. Each day is said to forecast the weather for the individual months ahead.

When the wind shifts against the sun, Trust it not for back 'twill run.

When the wind is in the east 'Tis neither good for man nor beast.

Mackerel sky and mares' tails Make the sailor furl his sails.

Watch the new moon. If you can hang a powder horn on the lower rim of the crescent, it is a sign of stormy weather.

The following are common signs of Rain: Soot falling to the ground, dogs sleeping through the day, spiders very active, rheumatic pains with elderly people.

To dream of horses is a sign with sailormen that storms will come.

When cats are very playful, they are said to "gale up the weather."

Folk Medicines

While some of Newfoundland folk medicines do not fall into the category of superstition, others definitely belong to the witch doctor domain. Their origins are diverse, and we can trace customs from continental Europe, England, Ireland, Scotland and the Channel Islands, and from Indian and Eskimo sources on this side of the Atlantic. Some oldtime remedies in which the use of herbs and balsams hold primary place indicate racial knowledge of medicinal properties. Others to which we call attention suggest that it may be worthwhile to explore their possibilities. In the latter class we may mention the use of alder buds and bark, the so-called "fish doctor," the use of maggots in the Eskimo poultice, and the curative properties of sea shells. We append some common remedies as practised in Newfoundland:

Stopping Blood
The application of cobwebs, also turpentine of fir. Nose bleed could be stopped by certain persons who recited a secret prayer or rite to achieve the desired effect.

Curing Warts
Cut notches in a stick and hide the latter. Rub a piece of fresh meat to the wart, then bury the meat and as it decayed the warts disappeared. Count the warts and make a like number of chalk marks on the back of a stove; as these burnt off the warts went also.

Toothache
Vinegar left in the mouth gave relief. Pebbles from the grave of a pious person provided a faith cure. The magician charmed away the toothache. One way to do this was to write some words on a scrap of paper and have the afflicted one carry the script on his person, but was forbidden to read it as the pain returned in punishment of such curiosity.

Hiccoughs
Distract the attention of the sufferer momentarily.

Pain In The Side
Put a pebble under the tongue.

Headache
Walk backwards, around in circle preferably.

Boils
A poultice of soap, flour and molasses on brown paper. To extract the core of a boil, put hot water in a bottle. Then empty the bottle and place its mouth on the boil; as the bottle cooled the core came out.

Infected Sores
Many people of Newfoundland recall some old resident of their community who was regarded as remarkable in healing festered sores. It was generally some motherly old lady who did the doctoring. Scorched linen, burnt cream, white of an egg, powdered dust of sea shells, dried and powdered seaweed, goose grease, mouldy bread – these are some of the ingredients of a good poultice.

Hernia
An old custom in order to cure a child of hernia was to split a green witch hazel tree and pass the child through it.

Stomach Trouble

The ground juniper boiled was supposed to be a panacea for stomach ills. Dogberry extract was also favourably regarded. Alder buds were also boiled and the extract used to good effect.

Hemorrhoids

Pine tar applied to the affected part produced relief.

Sore Eyes

May snow was gathered and bottled for a remedy. Many old people testify to the efficiency of this strange cure.

Incretions

Burnt ash of tobacco, powdered resin. Still used and approved by Newfoundland fisherfolk.

Nightmare

Locally known as the 'old hag." Call the person's name backwards.

Ingrowing Nails

Drop hot tallow from a lighted candle into the part affected, and instant relief was afforded.

Rheumatism

The great brown jellyfish was bottled, and when dissolved into fluid was rubbed to the affected parts and acted as a counter irritant. One objection to this cure was the offensive odour. The magician came to the rescue with an amulet of haddock fin which, worn on the neck, was a charm against rheumatic tendencies.

Cough

The most effective home remedies were extract of wild cherry and spirits of turpentine. Kerosene oil mixed with molasses proved effective. Snake root was also steeped for a cough medicine.

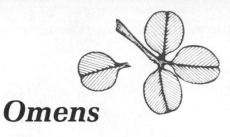

Omens

Good Luck

Seeing the new moon first over the left shoulder, picking up a horseshoe on the road, picking a four leaf clover, seeing two black crows flying overhead, putting on a garment inside out by mistake, picking up a coin, picking up a pin or a white button, a rooster crowing on the doorstep, to see a baby smiling in its sleep, to dream of one's father, a bee coming into the room.

Bad Luck

Breaking a mirror, having thirteen persons at table, coiling a rope against the sun, walking under a ladder, purchasing a broom in May, meeting a red haired woman, looking over another's shoulder into a mirror, coming in by one door and going out by another, meeting a cross-eyed person, to have a black cat cross your path, to spill salt, to cross knives on a table, to leave a knife turned blade upwards, to have a lone black crow fly over your head, to be called back just as you have begun a journey, to whistle on the water, to drop the ring at a marriage ceremony.

Death Tokens

A dog moaning near a house, a dog burying some object near one's home, a bird coming into a room, a clock which had been stopped for years suddenly striking the hours, a window blind falling without any apparent cause, a wall picture suddenly falling. When "rigor mortis" does not appear in a corpse it means that another member of the family will soon die. To dream of a wedding is a sign of a funeral. The banshee, a weird crying at night, is said to precede the death of certain persons of Irish descent in Newfoundland.

Tokens Good And Ill

A cat washing her face, sparks from a wood stove flying to the floor, a knife or fork falling, were regarded as tokens of a visit by a stranger. The first member of the assembled company at which the cat glared would be the first to die. Ringing in the ears betokened news, the right ear for good and the left for ill. To say things backwards betokened the sight of a long absent friend. It was considered taboo to step over a child, as this would stop the growth of the youngster. If a person had a cold spasm, it was said that someone was walking over the grave of the individual. It was considered very unlucky to incur the wrath of a widow, as her curse was sure to bring evil. An odd method of bringing ill fortune to an enemy was to throw the dust of one's shoes over the left shoulder in that person's direction. If things went badly on Monday, it was a sure sign of a bad week.

Quaint Beliefs And Practices

Maidens sought the name of their future husbands on the eve of Midsummer. They broke an egg and kept it in a glass, and spilled it on the road next morning. The first man to walk over the egg had the same Christian name as the husband-to-be. Belief in fairies was general; old folk still persist in vouching that they have seen these little fellows dancing on the grass on moonlit nights. Children lost in the woods were said to have been led astray by fairies; as a safeguard against this, every person carried a cake of hard biscuit in a pocket. Jack O'Lantern can still be seen on marshlands on calm nights; many believe that an evil spirit seeks to lure the unwary traveller astray. Fishermen's

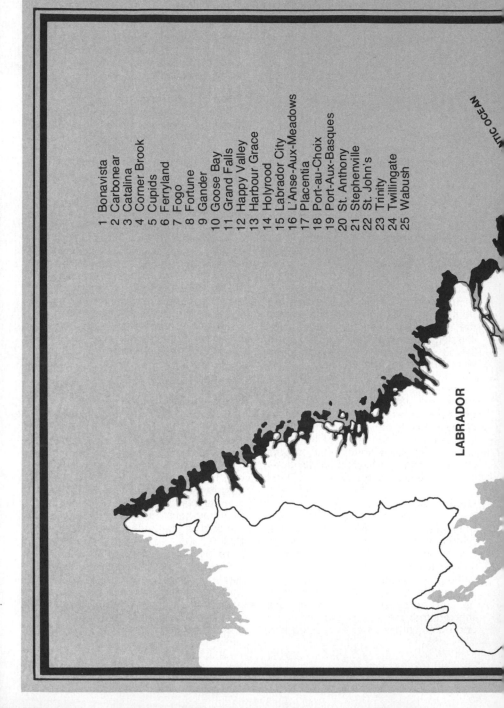

1 Bonavista
2 Carbonear
3 Catalina
4 Corner Brook
5 Cupids
6 Ferryland
7 Fogo
8 Fortune
9 Gander
10 Goose Bay
11 Grand Falls
12 Happy Valley
13 Harbour Grace
14 Holyrood
15 Labrador City
16 L'Anse-Aux-Meadows
17 Placentia
18 Port-au-Choix
19 Port-Aux-Basques
20 St. Anthony
21 Stephenville
22 St. John's
23 Trinity
24 Twillingate
25 Wabush

ATLANTIC OCEAN

LABRADOR

superstitions in boatbuilding are interesting. It was deemed necessary to have witch hazel in some part of the new craft, she was first turned with the sun, and it was lucky to have an old sail on her at the launching. Dead dogs were buried under fruit trees to ensure a good harvest. Sick calves had a peculiar knot tied over them. It was tied nine times and pulled clear; if it became tangled, the calf was certain to die.

Perhaps no part of the world is more productive of ghost stories than the island of Newfoundland. There we find in all their grim detail, handed down and enlarged from generation to generation, legends of the supernatural. They run the full gamut in the scale of horrors, from the ghost in the dark lane to the spectre who guards the pirate hoard and the phantom ships that appear with spectral crews. The church apparition, the graveyard with its walking dead, the cries of anguish from dark gulches where sailors went to their doom, the eerie light beyond the harbour bar, the shrieking hag beside the dark waterfall, the great black dog that emits fire from eyes and mouth, and shapeless creeping things in haunted houses with their nameless noises — all these and more the folk describe with bated breath and awesome tones. No doubt, imagination and exaggeration play a great part in these ghostly experiences and in their repeated recital. The phantom ship may be but a mirage, and St. Elmo's fire may be explained by natural causes, but the lure of the bizarre and supernatural can lead to things strange and startling.

Festal Customs

The feast of Christmas is celebrated in the Tenth Province in the good old fashioned way. Many Yuletide practices that were brought from Europe over three centuries ago are still found in Newfoundland. The custom of hauling the Yule Log through the village on Christmas Eve has disappeared but the time honoured practice of dressing as mummers is still in vogue even in the city of St. John's. One ancient rite that was popular a century ago in many outports was the performance of a play known as St. George and the dragon. A peculiar and pleasing practice still observed is the visit of young people to the baptismal sponsors on New Year's Day, to receive the latters' blessing and to partake of the traditional cakes and candy. Another ancient custom still carried on in the outports is the game of rounders. The ball is the bladder of a pig, encased in hairy bull hide, and a heavy club is used to propel the sphere to distant spaces. The game is played on the frozen surface of a lake if the ice is of sufficient strength, otherwise a level field is chosen as the scene of combat. This ancient game is regarded as the origin of the modern American baseball.

Other festal occasions are celebrated with gusto. On the night of November 5th huge bonfires are lit in every village to perpetuate the Guy Fawkes attempt to blow up the Parliament buildings in the time of James I. Green boughs and tar barrels are used to create a thick smoke screen, and through this dense pall of smoke young people dance and collide with shouts of laughter. Should a novice come in good clothes, he or she is marked for a lavish smearing of burnt embers. Other times of much merriment are Pancake Night, the eve of Lent, and the feast of St. Patrick. Old time dances are all in order on these occasions, and the music of the fiddle or the inevitable accordion gives the gay throng the necessary accompaniment. One glad interlude is the singing of some folk songs by some virtuoso or the dancing of a hornpipe by a professional heel and toe artist.

44

Placenames

Newfoundland has, perhaps, the most unusual collection of place names of any country in the world. The hackneyed manner by which other New World settlers identified their communities and natural landmarks did not appeal to the rugged types who settled here. Early day Newfoundlanders were, obviously, men of imagination and wit who were at their best when leaving place names to posterity.

Consider their humorous side. There must have been a twinkle in many an eye when such gems as these were bestowed:
Jerry's Nose
Nick's Nose Cove
Come-by-Chance
Blow-me-down
Lushes Bight
Bumble Bee Bight
Ha Ha Bay
Run-by-guess
Right-in-the-Run Island
Bleak Joke Cove
Calves Nose
Nancy Oh
Little Hooping Harbour
Snake's Bight
and, of course, *Joe Batt's Arm.*

On the other hand, it is not at all difficult to appreciate the depths of despair of those who experienced hardship or disaster on the rugged coastline. They gave to us such place names as:
Gripe Point
Bad Bay
Bleak Island
Misery Point
Famine Point
Wild Bight
Breakheart Point
Famish Gut
Savage Cove
Confusion Bay
Wreck Cove
Bareneed
and there's *Empty Basket.*

Then there were the happy contented settlers, whose satisfaction is reflected in such classics as:
Heart's Desire
Heart's Content
Safe Harbour
Heart's Delight
Comfort Cove
Little Heart's Ease
Sweet Bay
Too Good Arm
Little Paradise
Harbour Grace
Angel's Cove
and *Cupids.*

Although, there are no Londons, Parises or Birminghams in Newfoundland, there are place names which reflect the varied origins of the adventurers, colonists, soldiers, and traders who played a part in the Island's development:
English Harbour
Portugal Cove
Harbour Breton
Turk's Island
Frenchman's Cove
Jersey Harbour

45

*Canada Bay
and Ireland's Eye.*

The French who colonized a part of the Island and, later, held fishing rights for centuries, left a host of place names, some of which have lasted through years of mispronunciation by settlers of British origin:
*Bay D'Espoir (locally called and, sometimes written Bay Despair)
François
Bay de Vieux
Chaleur Bay
Cinq Cerf Bay
Beaubois
L'anse a l'Eau
and La Hune.*

Were the early settlers good house-keepers? They may have been, if the following place names have significance:
*Plate Cove
Grate's Cove
Ladle Cove
Spout Cove
Chimney Cove
Table Cove
Spoon Cove
Rooms
Bread Island
Cheese Island
Butter Cove
Tea Cove
Sugar Loaf
Cape Onion
Turnip Cove
Mutton Bay
Broom Point
Doughfig Point
Bacon Cove
Baker's Cove
Cook's Harbour
and Traytown.*

Apparently no one was colour blind in those far off days. At least, there are

many "Colourful" place names:
*Black Island
Red Island
Green Island
White Bay
Orange Bay
Blue Cove
Dark Cove
and Grey Islands.*

Geometricians of the day had their say with:
*Pyramid Point
Square Islands
Triangle Point
and Round Harbour.*

The animal world gets more than its fair share of mention in:
*Lion's Den
Bear's Cove
Horse Chops (!)
Hare's Ears Point
Cow Head
Dog Cove
Cat Gut
Little Cat Arm
Seal's Nest Island
Boar Point
Otter Point
Dragon Bay
Fox Roost
Muskrat Brook
and Goat Island.*

Bird life, too, has contributed a number of place names:
*Pigeon Island
Penguin Island
Turr Island
Black Duck
Gull Island
Goose Bay
Gander Bay
Swan Island
and Eagle Island.*

Of course, the fishermen who formed

the bulk of early settlers could be depended upon to name:
Caplin Cove
Trout River
Fishing Ship's Harbour
Herring Neck
Dog Fish Point
Boat Harbour
Steering Island
Schooner Island
Spudgels Cove
Rope Cove
Salmon Cove
Ship Cove
and Mooring Cove.

For the unimpressed (to this time) we may list:
Button Island
Shoe Cove
Stocking Harbour
and Petticoat Island.

Surprising as it may seem, the map shows:
Doctor's Harbour
Hatchet Cove
Sitdown Pond
and Goblin.

There's a False Cape and a Mistaken Point.

Religious feeling (or lack of it) probably accounts for place names such as:
God Bay
Sacred Bay
Devil Cove
and Nick's Nose Cove.

When all emotions and all imagination failed, even then early Newfoundlanders rose to the occasion. What better terms could be found than:
Nameless Cove
and Harbour Harbour.

It is, of course, impossible to list all the unusual place names in Newfoundand in a publication of this type. There are literally thousands of other names which are just as attractive (and some even more unusual) as those contained here. Many are in local usage only and cannot be found on any existing map.

The origin of many Newfoundland place names is a fascinating study in itself, and, at some time or other, nearly all her historians have devoted considerable time and research in an endeavour to explain just some of them.

Whether interest is academic or merely casual, however, the unique quality of our Provincial place names must fire the imagination of everyone, resident or visitor.

Folk Songs

Many old folk songs were brought to Newfoundland from England, Ireland and Scotland during more than three centuries of colonial growth. Apart from these there is another group that had its origin in the colonies on this side of the Atlantic, and there is a third aggregation that belongs solely to Newfoundland.

It is but a natural consequence that folk songs composed in Newfoundland should have as their main theme the experience of a race that has wrested its livelihood from the sea. Occasionally there are instances of other phases of life with these isolated people. There are love affairs, the eternal triangle, and the sense of loss by some lovelorn man or maiden. There are humorous situations, portrayed in a style all Newfoundland's own. There are even lullaby songs, composed from race experience and still crooned around the baby's cot. Much history has been written in songs that tell of outstanding events, of depression and failure of fisheries, and of the political animosities of party government. Many local sea shanties are parodies on the traditional British originals.

From the standpoint of literature it is rather difficult to evaluate Newfoundland folk songs. There is a certain amount of originality, and this is particularly true of the humorous songs of the John Burke type. In fact, it is difficult to find anywhere the prototype of Burke, as he most certainly touched the master key to success, the happy faculty of writing about something that nobody had previously attempted and of writing in a style altogether new. H. LeMessurier did not write many folk songs, but he immortalized "The Girl from Toslow." In our own day Scammel was inspired when he gave to the sons of Newfoundland for all time the rollicking rhyme of "The Squid Jiggin' Ground." There is simplicity in the Newfoundland folk songs, the simple stories of life, from out of the hearts of a kindly people. They are the creations of the soul of the race, and reveal the ethnic, aesthetic and historical background of an insular character.

The songs and airs published in this booklet were obtained through the kind co-operation of the late Gerald S. Doyle, O.B.E. Mr. Doyle was keenly interested in the folk songs of Newfoundland and made a lifetime hobby of collecting them. He published no less than three booklets which were distributed free of charge. Shortly before his death, permission was given to reproduce here the following songs, from the 1955 edition of "Old Time Songs of Newfoundland".

ODE TO NEWFOUNDLAND

Spiritoso

When Sun-rays crown thy pine-clad hills, And Sum-mer spreads her

allargando

hand, When sil-vern voi-ces tune thy rills We love thee smil-ing

rit.

land, We love thee, we love thee, we love thee, smil-ing land.

When blinding storm gusts fret thy
    shore,
And wild waves lash thy strand,
Thro' spindrift swirl and tempest
    roar,
We love thee wind-swept land,
We love thee, we love thee,
We love thee, wind-swept land.

When spread thy cloak of shimm'ring
    white,
At Winter's stern command,
Thro' shortened day and starlit night,
We love thee, frozen land,
We love thee, we love thee,
We love thee, frozen land.

As loved our fathers, so we love,
Where once they stood we stand,
Their prayer we raise to heav'n above,
God guard thee, Newfoundland
God guard thee, God guard thee,
God guard thee, Newfoundland.

— Sir Cavendish Boyle.

I'SE THE B'Y

Very rhythmically

1. I'se the b'y that builds the boat, And I'se the b'y that sails her!
2. Sods and rinds to cov - er yer flake, Cake and tea for sup - per,

I'se the b'y that catch-es the fish And takes 'em home to Li - zer.
Cod - fish in the spring o' the year Fried in mag-got-y but - ter.

CHORUS

Hip yer part - ner, Sal - ly Tibbo'! Hip yer part - ner, Sal - ly Brown!

Fo - go, Twil-lin-gate, Mor'- ton's Har - bour, All a - round the cir - cle!

I don't want your maggoty fish,
That's no good for winter;
I could buy as good as that
Down in Bonavista.

I took Lizer to a dance,
And faith, but she could travel'
And every step that she did take
Was up to her knees in gravel.

50

A GREAT BIG SEA HOVE IN LONG BEACH

A great big sea hove in the Harbour,
Right fol-or-all Ta-deedle, I do.
A great big sea hove in the Harbour,
And hove right up in Keough's Par-
    lour,
To me right fol didy fol dee.

Me boot is broke, me frock is tore,
Right fol-or-al Ta-deedle, I do;
Me boot is broke, me frock is tore,
But Georgie Snooks I do adore,
To me right fol didy fol dee.

Oh dear mother I wants a sack,
Right fol-or-al To-deedle, I do.
Oh dear mother I wants a sack
With beads and buttons all down the
    back,
To me right fol didy fol dee.

Oh fish is low and flour is high,
Right fol-or-al Ta-deedle, I do;
Fish is low and flour is high,
So Georgie Snooks he can't have I,
To me right fol didy fol dee.

But he will have me in the Fall,
Right fol-or-al Ta-deedle, I do;
If he don't I'll hoist my sail
And say good-bye to old Cannaille,
To me right fol didy fol dee.

SQUID-JIGGIN' GROUND

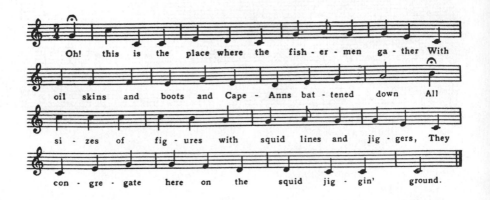

Oh! this is the place where the fish-er-men ga-ther With
oil skins and boots and Cape-Anns bat-tened down All
si-zes of fig-ures with squid lines and jig-gers, They
con-gre-gate here on the squid jig-gin' ground.

Some are workin' their jiggers while others are yarnin',
There's some standin' up and some more lyin' down,
While all kinds of fun, jokes and tricks are begun
As they wait for the squid on the squid-jiggin' ground.

There's men from the Harbour and men from the Tickle,
In all kinds of motor boats, green, gray and brown;
There's a red-headed Tory out here in a dory,
A runnin' down Squires on the squid-jiggin' ground.

There's men of all ages and boys in the bargain,
There's old Billy Chafe and there's young Raymond Brown;
Right younder is "Bobby" and with him is "Nobby",
They're a-chawin' hard tack on the squid-jiggin' ground.

The man with the whiskers is old Jacob Steele;
He's gettin' well up but he's still pretty sound;
While Uncle Bob Hawkins wears three pairs of stockin's
Whenever he's out on the squid-jiggin' ground.

52

God bless my sou'wester there's Skipper John Chaffey.
He's the best man at squid-jiggin' here, I'll be bound.
Hello! What's the row? Why, he's jiggin' one now—
The very first squid on the squid-jiggin' ground.

Holy smoke! What a bussel; all hands are excited.
It's a wonder to me that nobody is drowned.
There's a bussel, confusion, a wonderful hussel;
They're all jiggin' squid on the squid-jigging ground.

There's poor Uncle Billy, his whiskers are spattered
With spots of the squid juice that's flyin' around.
One poor little boy got it right in the eye
But they don't care a hang on the squid-jiggin' ground.

Says Bobby: "The squid are on top of the water
I just got me jigger about one fathom down"—
When a squid in the boat squirted right down his throat
And he's swearin' like mad on the squid-jiggin' ground.

Now if you ever feel inclined to go squiddin'
Leave your white shirt and collars behind in the town,
And if you get cranky without a silk hanky
You'd better steer clear of the squid-jiggin' ground.

— A. R. Scammel.
Used with the permission of
A. R. Scammel owner of Copyright.

LET ME FISH OFF CAPE ST. MARY'S

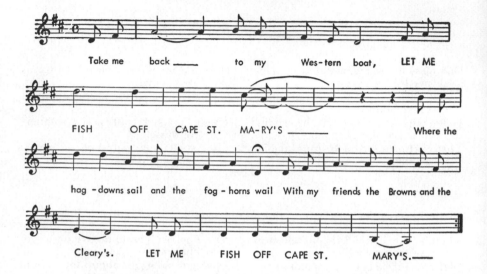

Take me back ___ to my Wes-tern boat, LET ME
FISH OFF CAPE ST. MA-RY'S ___ Where the
hag-downs sail and the fog-horns wail With my friends the Browns and the
Cleary's. LET ME FISH OFF CAPE ST. MARY'S.___

Let me feel my dory lift
To the broad Atlantic combers,
Where the tide rips swirl and the wild
    ducks whirl
Where Old Neptune calls the numbers
'Neath the broad Atlantic combers . . .

Let me sail up Golden Bay
With my oilskins all a'streamin' . . .
From the thunder squall — when I
    hauled me trawl
And my old Cape Ann a gleamin'
With my oil skins all a'streamin' . . .

Let me view that rugged shore,
Where the beach is all aglisten
With the caplin spawn where from
    dusk to dawn
You bait your trawl and listen
To the undertow a-hissin'.

When I reach that last big shoal
Where the ground swells break asun-
    der,
Where the wild sands roll to the surges
    toll.
Let me be a man and take it
When my dory fails to make it.

Take me back to the snug Green Cove
Where the seas roll up their thunder.
There let me rest in the earth's cool
    Breast
Where the stars shine out their wonder
And the seas roll up their thunder.

— Otto P. Kelland.

54

FELLER FROM FORTUNE

Oh,—Sally got a bouncin' new baby,
Father said that he didn't care;
Because he liked the Feller from Fortune,
What was down here fishin' last year.

Oh,—there's lots of fish in Bonavista Harbour,
Lots of fish right in around here;
Boys and girls are fishin' together,
Forty-five from Carbonear.

THE KELLIGREW'S SOIREE

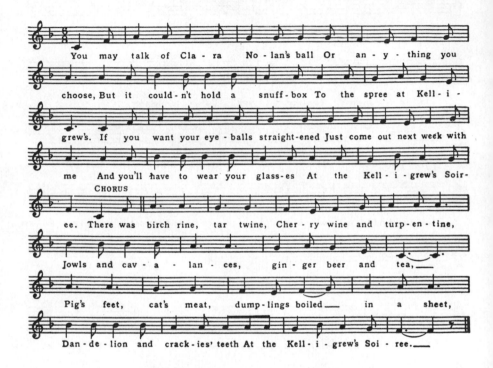

You may talk of Clara Nolan's ball Or anything you choose, But it couldn't hold a snuff-box To the spree at Kelligrew's. If you want your eye-balls straightened Just come out next week with me And you'll have to wear your glasses At the Kelligrew's Soiree.

CHORUS

There was birch rine, tar twine, Cherry wine and turpentine, Jowls and cavalances, ginger beer and tea, Pig's feet, cat's meat, dumplings boiled in a sheet, Dandelion and crackies' teeth At the Kelligrew's Soiree.

Oh, I borrowed Cluney's beaver,
As I squared my yards to sail;
And a swallow-tail from Hogan
That was foxy on the tail;
Billy Cuddahie's old working pants
And Patsy Nolan's shoes,
And an old white vest from Fogarty
To spot at Kelligrew's.

Chorus:

There was Dan Milley, Joe Lily,
Tantan and Mrs. Tilley,
Dancing like a little filly;
'Twould raise your heart to see.
Jim Brine, Din Ryan, Flipper Smith
    and Caroline;
.I tell you boys, we had a time
At the Kelligrew's Soiree.

Oh, when I arrived at Betsy Snooks'
That night at half past eight,
The place was blocked with carriages
Stood waiting at the gate,
With Cluney's funeral on my pate.
The first words Betsy said:
"Here comes a local preacher
With the pulpit on his head."

Chorus:

There was Bill Mews, Dan Hughes,
Wilson, Taft, and Teddy Roose,
While Bryant he sat in the blues
And looking hard at me;
Jim Fling, Tom King,
And Johnson, champion of the ring,
And all the boxers I could bring,
At the Kelligrew's Soiree.

The Saritoga Lancers first,
Miss Betsy kindly said;
Sure I danced with Nancy Cronan
And her Grannie on the "Head";
And Hogan danced with Betsey,
Oh, you should have seen his shoes,
As he lashed old muskets from the rack
That night at Kelligrews.

Chorus:

There was boiled guineas, cold guineas,
Bullocks' heads and picaninies,
And everything to catch the pennies,
You'd break your sides to see;
Boiled duff, cold duff, apple jam was in
    a cuff;
I tell you, boys, we had enough
At the Kelligrew's Soiree.

Crooked Flavin struck the fiddler
And a hand I then took in;
You should see George Cluney's be-
    aver,
And it flattened to the rim!
And Hogan's coat was like a vest —
The tails were gone you see,
Oh, says I "the devil haul ye
And your Kelligrew's Soiree."

— John Burke.

STAR OF LOGY BAY

♩.=66

Ye-la-dies and ye gen-tle-men, I-
pray you lend an ear ___ While I lo-
cate-the res-i-dence of a love-ly charm-er
fair. ___ The curl-ing of-her yel-low
locks First stole my heart a-way. And her place of
ha-bi-ta-tion Is-down in Lo-gy Bay. ___

It was on a summer's evening
This little place I found.
I met her aged father,
Who did me sore confound;
Saying: "If you address my daughter,
I'll send her far away,
And she never will return again
While you're in Logy Bay."

How could you be so cruel as
To part me from my love?
Her tender heart beats in her breast
As constant as a dove.
Oh, Venus was no fairer,
Nor the lovely month of May,
May Heaven above shower down its
love
On the Star of Logy Bay.

'Twas on the very next morning
He went to St. John's town
And engaged for a passage
In a vessel outward bound.
He robbed me of my heart's delight,
And sent her far away,
And left me here downhearted
For the Star of Logy Bay.

Oh, now I'll go a-roaming;
I can no longer stay.
I'll search the wide world over
In every country.
I'll search in vain thro' France and
Spain,
Likewise America
'Til I will sight my heart's delight
The Star of Logy Bay.

WRECK OF THE STEAMSHIP ETHIE

Words from Maude Roberts Simmonds, 1920

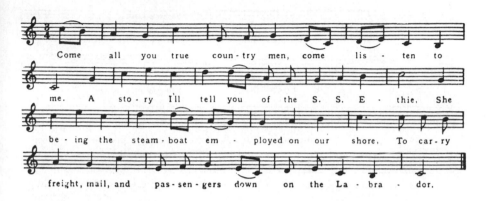

Come all you true coun-try men, come lis - ten to me. A sto-ry I'll tell you of the S. S. E - thie. She be - ing the steam-boat em - ployed on our shore, To car-ry freight, mail, and pas-sen-gers down on the La - bra - dor.

On the tenth of December, as you all
   well may know,
In the year nineteen nineteen, on her
   last trip did go;
Where she leaved Daniel's Harbour
   about 4 P.M.
With a strong breeze from the south-
   'ard, for Cow Head did steam.

The glass indicated a wild raging storm,
And about nine o'clock the storm did
   come on.
With the ship's husband on board, the
   crew had no fear;
Captain English gave orders straight
   for Bonne Bay to steer.

At first to the storm the brave ship gave
   no heed,
Until at length it was found she was fast
   losing speed,
And the great waves all round her like
   great mountains did rise,
And the crew all stood staring with fear
   in their eyes.

The orders went round to preserve for
   their life,
For the ship she is doomed and it's
   perish we might;
But still there is hope; there is one
   brave man on board
Who says he can guide her safely on to
   the shore.

Walter Young been our purser, as you
   may understand,
Volunteered for to guide her safely in
   to the land:
John Gullage, our first mate, bravely
   stood to the wheel;
Captain English gave orders and all
   worked with a will.

Up off Martin's Point about one
   o'clock,
Through bravery and courage, she es-
   caped every rock,
And the people on the shore saw the
   ship in distress;
All rushed to the spot for to help do
   their best.

And then we were landed in a rude
   boatswain's chair,
Taken in by the people and treated
   with care;
We stayed on the point until the storm
   it was o'er,
And the brave little *Ethie* lay standing
   on shore.

O, what of the fright, the exhaustion
   and cold,
The depth of my story will never be
   told!
And all you brave fellows gets ship-
   wrecked on the sea,
You thinks of the fate of the S.S. *Ethie*.

TICKLE COVE POND

In cuttin' and haul-in' in frost and in snow We're
up a-gainst trou-bles that few peo-ple know And
on-ly by pat-ience with cour-age and grit And eat-in' plain food can we
keep our-selves fit. The hard and the ais-ey we take as it comes, And
when ponds freeze o-ver we shor-ten our runs, To
hur ry my haul-ing___ the Spring com-ing on, Near

CHORUS

lost me my mare on Tick-le Cove Pond. Oh, lay
hold Will-iam Old-ford, lay hold Will-iam White, Lay hold of the cord-age and
pull all your might, Lay hold of the bow-line and
pull all you can, And give me a lift for poor Kit on the pond

60

I knew that the ice became weaker each
day,
But still took the risk and kept hauling
away,
One evening in April, bound home
with a load.
The mare showed some halting against
the ice road
And knew more than I did, as matters
turned out,
And lucky for me had I joined in her
doubt.
She turned 'round her head, and with
tears in her eyes,
As if she were saying. "You're risking
our lives."

I raised an alarm you could hear for a
mile
And neighbours turned up in a very
short while
You can always rely on the Oldfords
and Whites
To render assistance in all your bad
plights.
To help a poor neighbour is part of
their lives;
The same I can say of their children
and wives.
When the bowline was fastened around
the mare's breast
William White for a shanty song made a
request.

All this I ignored with a whip-handle
blow,
For man is too stupid dumb creatures
to know
The very next minute the pond gave a
sigh,
And down to our necks went poor Kitty
and I.

For if I had taken wise Kitty's advice
I never would take the short cut on the
ice
"Poor creature she's dead and poor
creature she's gone;
I'll never get my wood off Tickle Cove
Pond."

There was no time for thinking, no
time for delay,
So straight from his head came this
song right away:
"Lay hold William Oldford, lay hold
William White,
Lay hold of the hawser and pull all your
might,
Lay hold to the bowline and pull all you
can"
And with that we brought Kit out of
Tickle Cove Pond.

REPEAT CHORUS.

RYANS AND THE PITTMANS

We'll rant and we'll roar __ like true New-found-lan-ders We'll rant and we'll roar on deck and be-low Un-till we see bot-tom in-side the two sunk-ers When straight through the chan-nel to Tos-low we'll go.

I'm a son of a sea-cook, and a cook in a trader;
I can dance, I can sing, I can reef the mainboom,
I can handle a jigger, and cuts a big figure
Whenever I gets in a boat's standing room.

If the voyage is good, then this fall I will do it;
I wants two pound ten for a ring and the priest,
A couple o'dollars for clane shirt and collars,
And a handful o' coppers to make up a feast.

There's plump little Polly, her name is Goldsworthy;
There's John Coady's Kitty, and Mary Tibbo;
There's Clara from Bruley, and young Martha Foley,
But the nicest of all is my girl in Toslow.

Farewell and adieu to ye fair ones of Valen,
Farewell and adieu to ye girls in the Cove;
I'm bound to the Westward, to the wall with the hole in,
I'll take her from Toslow the wide world to rove.

Farewell and adieu to ye girls of St. Kyran's,
Of Paradise and Presque, Big and Little Bona,
I'm bound unto Toslow to marry sweet Biddy,
And if I don't do so, I'm afraid of her da.

I've bought me a house from Katherine Davis,
A twenty-pound bed from Jimmy McGrath;
I'll get me a settle, a pot and a kettle;
Then I'll be ready for Biddy — Hurrah!

I went to a dance one night at Fox Harbour;
There were plenty of girls, so nice as you'd wish;
There was one pretty maiden a-chawing of frankgum,
Just like a young kitten a-gnawing fresh fish.

Then here is a health to the girls of Fox Harbour,
Of Oderin and Presque, Crabbes Hole and Bruley.
Now let ye be jolly, don't be melancholy.
I can't marry all, or in chokey I'd be.

JACK WAS EVERY INCH A SAILOR

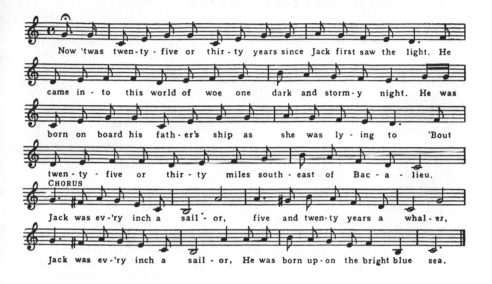

Now 'twas twen-ty - five or thir - ty years since Jack first saw the light. He
came in - to this world of woe one dark and storm-y night. He was
born on board his fath-er's ship as she was ly - ing to 'Bout
twen - ty - five or thir - ty miles south - east of Bac - a - lieu.

CHORUS

Jack was ev-'ry inch a sail'- or, five and twen-ty years a whal-er,
Jack was ev-'ry inch a sail - or, He was born up-on the bright blue sea.

When Jack grew up to be a man, he
  went to the Labrador.
He fished in Indian Harbour, where
  his father fished before.
On his returning in the fog, he met a
  heavy gale,
And Jack was swept into the sea and
  swallowed by a whale.

The whale went straight for Baffin's
  Bay, about ninety knots an hour.
And every time he'd blow a spray he'd
  send it in a shower.
"O, now," says Jack unto himself, "I
  must see what he's about."
He caught the whale all by the tail and
  turned him inside out.

REPEAT CHORUS.

Prehistoric People of Newfoundland and Labrador

The prehistory of Newfoundland and Labrador is long and fascinating. Archaeologists have found evidence of human habitation of the Province stretching back more than 9,000 years. Long before the coming of Europeans in the late 1400s there were Indian and Eskimo people living here, learning to use the resources of the land and the sea and developing the tools that they needed to survive.

The earliest evidence of human habitation in the Province comes from small campsites along the Strait of Belle Isle in southern Labrador. Only stone tools — spear or dart points, knives and small scrapers — have been preserved but, from the locations of the sites, archaeologists believe that these early people were hunting seals, caribou, sea birds and fishing for salmon. Charcoal from campfires has been dated to almost 9,000 years ago. These people spread gradually northward along the Labrador coast where they became more familiar with the resources of the area and how to exploit them. They eventually came to depend so heavily on the sea that their culture is known as the Maritime Archaic tradition.

Descendants of the early hunters of the Strait of Belle Isle may have reached northern Labrador as long as 6,000 years ago. By 5,000 years ago they had also moved south to colonize parts of the Island of Newfoundland. Archaeologists have found remains of their villages, campsites and burial places throughout the Province. At L'Anse-Amour, Labrador, a child about 12 years old was buried under a large pile of rocks about 7,500 years ago. This may be the oldest burial mound in the world. It has been restored as a provincial historic site and can be seen along the road to the community. Another fascinating burial site is the cemetery at Port au Choix, in western Newfoundland, where more than 100 people were buried between about 4,000 and 3,500 years ago. With the skeletons was a remarkable collection of weapons and tools as well as decorative and magical objects made from stone, bone, antler and ivory. The most impressive village site of these people is located in the far north of Labrador. Houses more than 50m long have been discovered at this site, as well as food caches, burials and a system of cairns designed to drive caribou toward the village where they could be killed for food and raw materials.

*F*rom these, and many other sites, archaeologists have reconstructed the culture of the Maritime Archaic people and have come to appreciate their inventiveness in coping with the sometimes harsh environment of Newfoundland and Labrador. They appear to have spent most of the year near the coast where they hunted seals, wal-

rus and perhaps other sea mammals. They also fished for salmon and hunted all species of sea birds, including the now-extinct Great Auk. Caribou, beaver and other land animals were also important to these people, both for food and as a source of furs and raw materials for tools and weapons.

The sea and its resources seem to have been of paramount importance to the Maritime Archaic people. This is known from their choice of campsites and from the foods they ate. It is also reflected in their art, which includes representations of whales and many types of sea birds. It is also seen in the magical charms and amulets which they carried, in some cases to their graves, which included the claws of seals, whales' teeth, and the heads, feet and skins of many species of sea birds. Many of these objects can be seen at the interpretation centre at Port au Choix and at the Newfoundland Museum.

*A*bout 4,000 years ago a people with a language, culture and history distinct from the Maritime Archaic tradition appeared on the northern Labrador coast. They were people from the Canadian Arctic to whom archaeologists refer as Palaeo-Eskimos. The first Palaeo-Eskimo people used tools and weapons of wood, antler, bone, ivory stone and other materials, but in most cases only the stone tools and weapons have been preserved. The minute stone tools and weapons made by these people are among the finest ever made. They are flaked from colourful fine-grained stone and are so exquisitely manufactured that they have an almost jewel-like quality. Although the tools and weapons were used for many of the same purposes as those of the Maritime Archaic people, they are very different in almost every respect.

These early Palaeo-Eskimos eventually travelled as far south as the Island of Newfoundland and their sites have been recorded from virtually every region of the coast. Then, slightly before 2,000 years ago, they just disappear from the archaeological record, perhaps victims of changing environmental conditions.

About 2,500 years ago a new group of Palaeo-Eskimos, usually called Dorset Eskimos, appeared in northern Labrador. Just as their earlier cousins had done some 1,500 years previously they, too, spread throughout the Province. Their campsites and villages have been discovered on almost every part of the Labrador and Newfoundland coasts. Their tools and weapons of chipped stone exhibit many of the same characteristics as those of their predecessors. In some places, bone, antler and ivory have been found made into harpoons, sled shoes, stylized carvings of seals and bears and other useful and decorative objects. In northern Labrador soapstone carvings of miniature bears, shells, human figures and other objects have been recovered. By about A.D. 1,000 the Dorset people appear to have followed the Palaeo-Eskimos into extinction. Only in northern Labrador did Dorset people persist for a few hundred more years.

While these people subsisted on many of the same species as had the Maritime Archaic Indians, many of their tools and weapons were markedly different. Their houses, too, were distinctive. A large Dorset Eskimo village near Port au Choix had more than 40 houses walled with sod and probably covered with a wood frame and hide roof. Remains of this large village, perhaps occupied for as many as 500 years, are still visible today. Artifacts from all Palaeo-Eskimo cultures are on display at the Newfoundland Museum in St. John's.

The Palaeo-Eskimo migration into Newfoundland and Labrador displaced many Indian peoples. In northern Labrador and on the Island of Newfoundland archaeologists have been unable to find any traces of the Maritime Archaic after about 3,500 yars ago. In southern Labrador, however, and on parts of the central Labrador coast, some Maritime Archaic people seem to have survived throughout the Palaeo-Eskimo period. What remains of their culture is much changed. The elaborate polished stone tools and weapons and the lavish ochre-covered burials of earlier times are no longer found. Instead, simple stone tools — projectile points, knives, scrapers and so forth — are all that remain. These are found scattered around small hearths in coastal locations, so it is believed that marine hunting and fishing remained important subsistence activities. Archaeologists have been able to trace these people forward in time until the arrival of the first Europeans. Some scholars believe that these coastally-adapted people may have been the ancestors of the Montagnais-Naskapi people who inhabit parts of the Labrador Peninsula today.

Around 2,000 years ago Indian people again appear in the archaeological record on the Island of Newfoundland. Whether these people migrated to the island at this time or were actually present since the Maritime Archaic demise remains a mystery. They do seem to have lived on the island throughout the Dorset Eskimo period and must have had some contact with those people After the disappearance of the Dorset Eskimos, evidence of Indian cultures becomes much more evident and it is probably safe to say that by A.D. 1,000 the ancestors of the Beothuk Indians had emerged.

*E*vidence from a series of sites indicates that the ancestors of the Beothuk lived along the coast just as their Archaic predecessors had. Their projectile points, probably arrowheads, knives, small scrapers and other stone tools and weapons show gradual changes through time until the historic period when they begin to be replaced by corresponding tools made from iron and other European materials. In the face of European pressure, their coastal pit-house villages were eventually abandoned and the Beothuk of the later historic period attempted to exist in the interior of Newfoundland, particularly along the Exploits River where their most recent campsites date to the early nineteenth century.

The last prehistoric people to arrive in the Province were the so-called Thule Eskimos, ancestors of the present-day Inuit of the Labrador coast. Before contact with Europeans they lived in sod-covered winter houses, dug partly into the ground and framed with the bones of right and bowhead whales which they were able to kill offshore. Besides whale meat, their diet consisted of a variety of seals, walrus, fish, birds and land mammals which they hunted with harpoons, spears, bows and arrows or captured with snares and traps. Their other equipment included most of that generally found among prehistoric Canadian Inuit — dog sleds and harnesses, "kayaks" and "umiaks", the snow knife, and objects which indicate their ingenious adaption to northern conditions. Although the Labrador Inuit have been in contact with Europeans for more than 400 years and many aspects of their culture are greatly changed, a surprising amount of the native way of life remains and can be seen by travellers to the Labrador coast.

This summary of Newfoundland and Labrador's prehistory is far from complete, This is not only because of its brevity, but also because there are a great number of questions for which answers have not yet been found. Archaeological investigations take place each summer and piece by piece the puzzle of our prehistory is taking shape. Many of these excavations are open to the public and visitors are invited to stop by and watch as the past is revealed.

The Beothuks

At the time of European expansion and settlement in Newfoundland, the Beothuks were the native inhabitants of the Island. The traditional pattern of life for these Indians disintegrated with the advent of this new influx of people, the Europeans and the Micmacs from Nova Scotia.

Although initial contacts between these people are recorded as being friendly, misunderstanding and suspicion increased to the point where actual killings occurred on both sides for real or

imaginary injustices.

Finally, starvation was added when the increasing numbers of Europeans unknowingly blocked the Beothuks access to the coast and to their traditional livelihood. By the early 1800's these people had disappeared as a distinct cultural group.

Research on the Beothuks during the past decade has enabled a partial reconstruction of their culture, language and traditional pattern of life that the tragic historic period closed so quickly and forever.

The Beothuks were hunters and took full advantage of the abundant food resources on the Island. These food resources were available seasonally, either on the sea coast or the interior forests and barrens. Two major movements or migrations were made in a given year to these areas to hunt and gather their resources.

Spring and summer were spent on the coast hunting the seals, whales, and other sea mammals that were extremely numerous during these seasons. The thousands of shore and seabirds, with their eggs, undoubtedly were another major resource while on the coast. With the arrival of fall the family groups, spread along the shoreline, moved inland, attracted by the caribou that were now herding together and migrating by the hundreds.

It is likely that the family groups coalesced for this caribou hunt and the maintenance of the "deer fences" that are reported to have stretched for miles. These fences funneled the migrating herds into one area where they could be more easily speared. These animals provided skins for clothing and shelter, and meat for subsistence during the remaining winter. Small game such as beaver, fox and ptarmigan supplemented their food supply during these months.

With spring, there was a return to the coast and its resources, which were again becoming available at this time. These movements were probably facilitated by the use of the large river systems such as the Exploits, Gander and Terra Nova.

Structures for shelter at these coastal and interior hunting camps are partially known from early historic accounts and by archaeological excavations.

In the winter, shelter was provided by "mamateeks". These conical structures consisted of a framework of straight poles meeting in the centre, where a passage was left for smoke to escape. This was covered by layers of skin, birch bark and, in several reports, by sail cloth obtained from the Europeans. Finally, soil was banked against the mamateek along the outside, effectively sealing it against the elements.

At several archaeological sites this external banking of soil provided the outline of the mamateek and showed a multi-sided structure where the banking stretched from one frame pole to the next. One such excavation at Red Indian Lake revealed a six-sided mamateek measuring twenty-five feet by twenty feet. A large interior hearth provided warmth and cooking facilities during the winter months. Towards one end was a platform which may have served as a storage area. Around the hearth were several long depressions or hollows which served as an individual's sleeping area.

Another site on the Exploits River revealed a similar multi-sided mamateek. Around this winter lodging were several rock and bone mash concentrations. These rock concentrations may have been used for sweat baths or simply a redeposition of rocks taken from the interior hearth of the mamateek. The bone mash results from the boiling of split caribou bones in order to extract the marrow and oil. Heat was provided by dumping red-hot granite cobbles into the water-filled vessel. Once the oil was skimmed from the top, the remaining rocks, bone mash and water were dumped aside to be discovered and interpreted by the archaeologists centuries later.

Coastal structures are not described adequately in any of the historic records. The archaeological findings to date only partially clarify this lack of data. At one site, in Bonavista Bay, four circular depressions ranging from twelve to twenty-three feet in diameter were located. Again, it was the exterior banking of soil that provided an outline of the structure. In these cases they appear to be of a circular construction. The structural difference from interior sites may be due to the less severe climatic demands of a summer occupation, and perhaps a smaller social grouping at this time of year.

Subsistence of this coastal site was primarily based on seals, including young harbour seals available in the spring. Also identified in the refuse bone concentration found outside one structure were sea duck, cormorant and black bear. These indicated that the Beothuks occupied this site through the summer and possibly early fall to obtain these various food resources.

At these interior and coastal habitation sites, items used in their everyday existence are usually found. Unfortunately because of the poor preservability of wood and bone tools in the soil over the centuries, the items so far uncovered consist entirely of stone artifacts. These are predominantly spear and arrowheads reflecting their hunting activities. Some scrapers were also

found and these served to prepare hides and skins for their eventual use as clothing, decoration and shelter.

Actual examples of the highly perishable items have only been found in Beothuk burials. These have been preserved by having been smeared with a mixture of red ochre and grease which has acted as a natural preservative.

From the various Beothuk burials we have examples of leather clothing with frills; birch bark vessels, sometimes with decorative stitching and notched edges; pendants which are elaborately carved and incised bone and ivory pieces that stylistically are unique to these people; and in one burial a wooden carving representing a male Indian.

Occasionally, materials obtained from the European fishermen and settlers are also included alongside the body. These metal knives, nails, sword and clay pipes indicate that the Beothuks were in contact with the early French as well as English sailors.

Reconstruction of Beothuk religious beliefs remains highly speculative. Various ceremonies must have occurred to bring good hunting, successful child birth or restoration of health. It is only in their mortuary practices, in the preparation and care given to the deceased, that we have tangible evidence of a spiritual belief.

Beothuk burials so far uncovered are almost exclusively located in coastal caves or rock shelters located along the numerous bays around the Island. In a few instances there are reports of there being stone-lined crypts within these caves and a birch canopy on poles above the burial. Red ochre is used lavishly over the body and bones and is symbolic to many cultures as a life-giving force. The items which are included beside the body are also covered with this ochre. These finely made pieces provide us with valuable artifacts of the Beothuk culture. The physical remains in these burials do not clarify the often-mentioned lore that these Indians were of great stature and height. To date, the numerous burials found by archaeologists have all been previously disturbed burials. The skeletons have been too scattered and fragmentary for proper analysis as to stature, age or sex.

One notable exception is the fairly complete skeleton of a male Beothuk Indian presently in the Newfoundland Museum collection. This represents an exceptional individual probably having been close to 6 feet in height.

However, both John Guy, who established the first English colony in Newfoundland in 1610 and Lieut. David Buchan R.N., who had numerous encounters with the Beothuks in the early 1800's, describe them differently. They are characterized by both these explorers as being of average height, light brown skin and dark hair and eyes. Buchan made further note of the fact that they smeared their bodies and clothing with red ochre and grease. This custom is mentioned in several historic accounts and appears to be the origin for calling the Beothuks the "Red Indians".

Two Beothuk women, Demasduit and Shanawdithit, are known from the early nineteenth century. They were not of exceptional height and certainly are within the description given by John Guy and David Buchan.

The names of these two women, Demasduit, or Mary March, and Shanawdithit, or Nancy, are well-known to Beothuk researchers. Both lived among the settlers in various communities and are the sources of invaluable information on items of Beothuk culture that had previously been unobtainable. Nancy, in particular, provided drawings illustrating various foods used and stored by her people, a winter dwelling or mamateek, and various mythological items. There are even several drawings dealing with the encounters of her people with Europeans at Red Indian Lake.

Probably the most important items obtained independently from these women were the lists of words which form two vocabularies of their language. These remain critical clues in the identification of these people and are the basis for their linguistic Algonkian association.

Indeed, the growing archaeological, enthological and linguistic evidence indicates that the Beothuk formed linguistically and culturally a part of the widely distributed Algonkian continuum presently spread across the maritime area of eastern Canada.

*T*he identification of their prehistoric cultural ancestors and time of their ultimate appearance in Newfoundland remains inconclusive. Archaeological investigators have revealed the prehistoric occupation of insular Newfoundland to consist of multiple occupations by several cultural groups. These included the earliest Maritime Archaic Indians, the Dorset Eskimos and finally those Indians known during the recent European occupation as the Beothuks.

There is growing awareness of the possibility of their descending from the earliest Maritime Archaic Indians. If this is ultimately proven, the Beothuks would represent the historically known descendents of an Indian group whose occupation of Newfoundland was continuous from its inception many thousands of years ago.

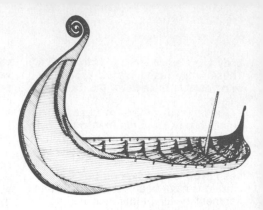

The Vikings
In Newfoundland

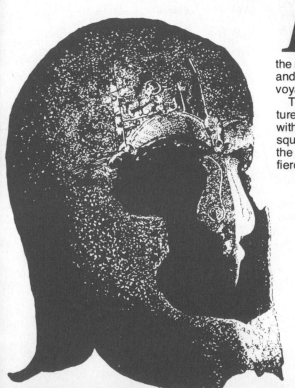

Few periods in the history of mankind can evoke more colourful imagery than the era when the bold and warlike Vikings dominated the maritime regions of Northern Europe and sailed out of Scandinavian ports on voyages of exploration and colonization.

There springs to mind a dramatic picture of the high-prowed "long ships," with sweeping oars supplementing the square woolen sails. Battle shields line the gunwales and behind them are the fierce Viking warriors, clad in garments of leather and fur with horned metal helmets glinting in the sun. Their reputation as savage and reckless warriors terrorized the foreign lands chosen as targets for their expeditions and few victims withstood the ferocity of their forays of conquest. As they developed larger and sturdier ships, the Viking rovers ventured further and further West, to the Shetlands, Orkneys and Faeroe Islands and eventually to Iceland.

Once they had reached Iceland and established stable communities there, it was to be only a matter of time before bold spirits among them sought new horizons to the westward.

Eric the Red was the son of Thorvald, who, as an exiled murderer, fled from Norway to Iceland. Eric himself incurred similar punishment and in 982 he fled from Iceland, after telling friends he would look for the land that an earlier voyager had sighted farther westward. He reached an ice-rimmed coast which he explored for several years before returning to Iceland, where he reported finding a good land. With the hope of luring settlers, he named his discovery Greenland. The following year, Eric led an expedition carrying all the basic requirements for serious colonization. The newcomers built houses of stone and turf in the fiords of Greenland's Southwest coast, creating settlements which apparently survived for about 500 years.

When Bjarni Herjulfesson left Iceland, soon after 986, to join his father in Greenland, he was driven far Southwest by bad weather. He sighted unfamiliar coasts but without landing anywhere he turned back out to sea and eventually reached Greenland.

*L*eif Eiriksson, son of Eric the Red, was prompted by Bjarni's findings to organize an expedition. He reached the far North land Bjarni had seen, very probably Baffin Island, and gave it the name Helluland (land of flat stones).

Turning southward, he found low, forested coastline with white sand beaches. This was apparently Labrador and Leif named it Markland (Woodland). He finally arrived at a third place which tempted the seafarers with good grazing ground, timber and salmon. The Sagas tell us that Leif built large houses there and he "gave the land a name in accordance with the good things they found in it, calling it Vinland." After remaining a year or so he returned to Greenland.

The glowing account of Vinland or "Vineland the Good" encouraged others to mount expeditions to the new country which Leif had found. None of them achieved permanent settlement and each group eventually returned to Greenland. The wife of one of the colonists, Thorfinn Karlsefni, brought back with her a small boy named Snorri, the first European born in North America.

Historians who have studied the Viking Sagas have tried to identify the actual locations visited and settled by the adventurous Vikings of long ago. All have long accepted as fact that the Norsemen reached America but the fascinating question has been the exact site of Vinland the Good.

The Sagas, partly by allusions to relatively short sailing routes to America, indicate that Vinland was a Northern place. Many scholars, however, have believed that "Vin" referred to wild grapes, indicating that Vinland would be farther south on the Atlantic Coast, somewhere in what is now known as the New England area.

Others were convinced that "Vin" in Vinland had nothing to do with grapes but instead was used in the old Norse sense of "grass" or grazing lands. Thus given wider scope, they favoured a location somewhere along the coast of Newfoundland or Labrador.

ore than a half century ago, the published findings of W. A. Munn, a distinguished Newfoundland historian, presented a very convincing case identifying the general area of Pistolet Bay at the northern tip of the island of Newfoundland as the site of Vinland the Good. More specifically, he visualized the Vikings landing at what is now known as L'Anse-aux-Meadows and then sailing around Cape Onion into Pistolet Bay to settle on the shores of Milan Arm.

It is extremely interesting to note that his theories placed a Viking settlement within a few scant miles of the spot where, 50 years later, archaeologists unearthed actual evidence of a Norse village. The recent findings were made at L'Anse-aux-Meadows, mentioned in Mr. Munn's account as one of the temporary landing places of the Vikings.

In the Spring of 1960, a twentieth century Viking explorer appeared in Newfoundland. Helge Ingstad, a tall, white-haired Norwegian, has spent most of his adult life in scientific research and exploration and has published a number of comprehensive books on the ancient history of Northern and Arctic civilizations.

Because of his own nationality, his most abiding dedication was to his long and painstaking research into the mystery of the earliest Greenland colonists and the fate of their various expeditions to lands in the Western reaches of the North Atlantic.

In common with a number of other scholars, Helge Ingstad interpreted the Icelandic Sagas in such a way as to suggest that "Vinland the Good" was very probably somewhere in Newfoundland or Labrador. His systematic search for evidence had already taken him to Rhode Island, Massachusetts and Nova Scotia.

After preliminary surveys in 1960, Ingstad returned in 1961 with a fully organized exploration party. By plane and boat, travelling almost 4000 miles, he and his associates carried out a close and intensive study of the coast of Newfoundland and Labrador and their investigations eventually led them to L'Anse-aux-Meadows.

Attracted by faint outlines in the surface contours of the land, they began careful excavation work under the direction of Mrs. Anne Stine Ingstad, who is a trained archaeologist. They found remains which suggested the walls of very old buildings, seven in all, including a layout resembling a great hall in the Viking style.

Anne Stine Ingstad also discovered a little fireplace lined with slate, a cooking pit and traces of a hearth. At the outer edge of the hearth was found a slate-lined recess measuring about 6½ by 10 inches. This was identified as an "ember pit" where a few hot coals were kept alive at night, covered with ashes, ready to start the breakfast fire next morning. Similar ember pits have been excavated at several Greenland farms, including Brattahlid, the homestead of Eric the Red.

*I*n 1962-64, Ingstad organized new expeditions during which excavation and research disclosed further details of the ancient settlement. The big house was found to have measured 70 by 55 feet, with five or six rooms and several fireplaces. In most of the buildings the lower walls consisted of turf; the upper walls and roof were probably of wood.

Several of the houses contained lumps of iron slag and the researchers discovered rich deposits of bog iron, caked on the bottom of the turf turned over by their shovels. Icelandic scientists with the party, led by D. Kristjan Eldjarn, excavated some depressions in the banks of the stream which runs by the site and found hundreds of pieces of slag, together with a large, flat-surfaced stone and traces of a fireplace. Everything points to the conclusion that the stone had served as an anvil in a primitive smithy. To run a smithy required charcoal and the Icelanders found a thick layer of charred wood in another pit close to the location of the smithy.

When later tested by the scientific radiocarbon dating method the material in the blacksmith's fireplace gave two readings. One was AD 860 plus or minus 90 years and the other AD 1060 plus or minus 70 years.

Three years of digging at L'Anse-au-Meadow brought the major field work to completion but in 1964 further work was done to stabilize the excavations and ruins and repair any winter damage.

While working under Mrs. Ingstad's direction, Tony Beardsley, a young Canadian helper, dug through the turf to a layer black with scattered charcoal. Here, on August 4, 1964, he found a tiny stone wheel which ranks as one of the great archaeological discoveries in North America.

It is 1¼ inches in width and carved from soapstone. Technically, it is called a spindle whorl and served as a fly wheel on a wool spinning spindle. Many similar implements have been found at Norse sites in Greenland, Iceland and Norway and it indicates that the settlers at L'Anse-aux-Meadows included women, who attended to household tasks while their husbands sought unsuccessfully to carve a permanent settlement in Vinland some 500 years before the voyages of Columbus. After so many years of speculation and controversy among scholars and historians, the findings at L'Anse-aux-Meadows take on enormous importance.

The leader of the expeditions, Helge Ingstad, has carefully avoided making any specific claim relating the site to Leif Eiriksson or any other individual Viking. It is unlikely that the actual identity of the colonists can ever be fully determined. There is a strong possibility that the Norse voyagers established settlements at other points along the coast of Newfoundland and adjacent territories. The importance of L'Anse-aux-Meadows lies in the fact that it is the only place where actual evidence that withstands scientific scrutiny has been found.

The Portuguese In Newfoundland Waters

The sheltered harbour of St. John's has provided a safe haven for ships of many nations for more than four centuries. The colourful array of foreign vessels moored two and three abreast along the waterfront makes a fascinating sight when storm warnings on the Grand Banks call a halt to fishing and cause the ships to seek the safety of the strategically located and virtually landlocked port.

Prominent among them are the sturdy vessels of the "White Fleet" of Portugal, which has been sending ships to the Grand Banks of Newfoundland since the earliest years of the recorded history of the areas. The Portuguese share the hospitality of St. John's with sailors and fishermen from France, Spain, Norway, Russia, Germany and Great Britain, since virtually all of the maritime nations on both sides of the Atlantic exploit the prolific fishery of the Grand Banks, a submarine plateau or continental shelf which commences about fifty miles east of Cape Race, Newfoundland.

When John Cabot returned from his voyage of discovery in 1497, his reports of the abundance of cod to be found in the coastal waters of Newfoundland aroused the eager interest of the fishing merchants in the east of England. They persuaded the Crown to impose harsh anti-settlement laws which held back any appreciable colonization of the "New Founde Lande" for centuries after its discovery.

Although the repressive laws prevented legal settlement by colonists from Great Britain, they could do nothing to discourage other countries from sharing in the fishing bonanza to be found on the Grand Banks.

The fifteenth and sixteenth centuries saw the beginning of Portuguese exploration, backed by the maritimes ingenuity which took adventurous navigators from Portugal to many far-distant corners of the world.

Some of their names are widely known — Prince Henry, Magellan and Vasco de Gama — and are readily recognized by any reasonably well-read persons. Others are less familiar except to serious students of history. The brothers Gaspar and Miguel Corte Real made bold voyages seeking the elusive North West Passage in tiny caravels of the Order of Christ in the years 1501-1502. Miguel was lost in the northern seas while seeking his brother Gaspar, who is credited by some historians with explorations of the coasts from Greenland all the way to New England.

*T*wo other Portuguese, Alvarex Fagundes and Estevan Gomez (the latter serving Spain) navigated, respectively, the Gulf of St. Lawrence and the Bay of Fundy before 1525, more than a decade ahead of the well-documented voyages of Jacques Cartier. In recognition of the contribution made by the Corte Real brothers, the King of Portugal granted to their brother Vasco and his descendants "Real and actual possession of the Mainland and Islands" discovered by Gaspar Corte Real during the expeditions which were financed and carried out by this Azores family at tremendous material and physical cost. Fagundes, in 1520, applied for and received a nominal royal grant of the lands he might discover "within the Portuguese sphere of influence". Some of the names he gave to points he discovered in the western part of Newfoundland were later changed to English and French nomenclature.

It has been asserted by some historians that the Portuguese were the first to exploit the fishing found on the Grand Banks, late in the 15th century. In support of this theory there is documentation of special tithes levied on catches of cod by King Manuel of Portugal as early as 1506. For a century or more after its recorded discovery, Newfoundland became known to Western Europe as "Tierra dos Bacallaos" (Portuguese for codfish). It is identified in this manner on a map published in 1569 by the celebrated Dutchman Gerardus Mercator, who marked Labrador (the Portuguese word for farmer) as "Terra Corte Realis".

Some of the longest settled and most historic parts of the Island of Newfoundland still bear names of Portuguese origin, since many of the 16th century cartographers were Portuguese and were the first to assign names to the major capes, bays, harbours and islands on the east and southeast coasts of Newfoundland. As early as 1502 a Portuguese map identified what is now Newfoundland as "Land of the King of Portugal".

Despite the various nominal royal grants of land to the early Portuguese explorers, there appears to be no appreciable evidence of any organized or determined attempt to confirm territorial claims or ambitions by military or naval force or by planned colonization. Along with some of the other seafaring nations, Portugal continued to send fishing fleets to the Grand Banks on a seasonal basis. The principal port, St. John's, became familiar to succeeding generations of sailors and fishermen from the various fishing countries of the world and has retained its identity on an international level for more than four centuries.

*F*rom May to October each year, the ships of Portugal's "White Fleet" lend unique colour and charm to the port of St. John's. Until the 1950's, these ships were of the traditional bank fishing schooner design, with decks piled high with colourful wooden dories. They have been replaced by modern draggers and trawlers.

The most conspicuous aspect of the long association of Portugal with Newfoundland has been the virtually complete absence of any serious friction to mar the mutually friendly relationship shared by the many hundreds of fishermen and the resident population of St. John's. It is a remarkable tribute to the rugged, hard-working men of the Portuguese fleets that so many thousands of them have staged their friendly invasion of Newfoundland's provincial capital at frequent intervals throughout the summer months and maintained an unrivalled reputation for good behaviour that has kept them in high standing as extremely welcome visitors.

On two occasions in recent years, the special relationship between Newfoundland and Portugal has been given official public recognition. In 1955, the Roman Catholic Cathedral in St. John's observed its centennial and was evaluated to the rank of Basilica. A highlight of the celebrations was a parade of several thousand Portuguese fishermen who marched through the city from the waterfront to the Basilica and presented an enduring gift in the form of a statue of Our Lady of Fátima. Again, in 1965, they gathered in large numbers for the ceremonial unveiling of a huge bronze statue of Gaspar Corte Real erected in a prominent location on Prince Philip Drive adjacent to Confederation Building, headquarters of the Provincial Government.

The statue stands on a large concrete platform, on which is engraved in large letters an inscription which bears testimony to an historic international friendship; it reads "Gaspar Corte Real, Portuguese Navigator. He reached Terra Nova in the 15th. century at the beginning of the era of the great discoveries. From the Portuguese Fisheries Organization as an expression of gratitude on behalf of the Portuguese Grand Banks Fishermen for the friendly hospitality always extended to them by the people of Terra Nova — May 1965".

Basque Whalers in Southern Labrador 1540-1610

During the latter half of the sixteenth century Basque whalers from northeastern Spain and southwestern France conducted a profitable whale hunt each summer in southern Labrador. While more than a dozen whaling ports are known, the most important of these was located at what is now Red Bay. Archaeologists have been working on land and under the waters of the bay since 1977 to uncover the remains of the shore stations where whale blubber was processed into marketable oil and the wrecks of a number of ships and boats from the sixteenth century.

Underwater archaeologists have excavated completely a whaling galleon of about 300 tonnes. It is believed to be the "San Juan" which sank with a full cargo of whale oil late in the year 1565, just as it was ready to sail for Spain. Remains of the cargo of barrels, now collapsed upon themselves, as well as the ship itself were remarkably preserved by the cold waters of Red Bay Harbour. Divers have recovered large portions of the hull, the capstan, bits of rigging — including almost perfectly preserved hemp ropes and wooden blocks —, a compass and other navigational instruments. There were also a large number of personal possessions

of the ship's crew discovered in the wreck. These included shoes, baskets, ceramic vessels and a variety of other objects. One of the most interesting finds is a carving of a ship, somewhat roughly done on a softwood plank, which may be a representation of the "San Juan" herself.

Scattered around the wreck were the bones of whales which had been killed during the late sixteenth century and a thick layer of codfish bones of exactly the same kind as those discarded by present-day fishermen when preparing cod for salting. Also found near the underwater site were the remains of several small boats, about eight metres long and with positions for oarsmen. They are almost certainly the remains of the small vessels from which whales were hunted. They were, in many respects, similar to the more recent, and more famous, New England whaleboats of the eighteenth and nineteenth centuries.

These wrecks were located close to one of the shore stations and surveys in other parts of the harbour have revealed two more large vessels and a smaller "pinnace", about 40 feet long which may have been used to travel from harbour to harbour during the Basque whaling period.

The large ships did not actually figure in the whaling. They were moored in the harbours and served as floating warehouses for the refined oil. The hunt took place from small boats, in a fashion very similar to that of later periods. The whales were then towed ashore to stations located along the harbour edge.

These shore stations consisted of a number of tile-roofed buildings where industrial activities were carried out. A wharf or "cutting-in" stage extended into the water and it was here that right and bowhead whales were stripped of their blubber. It was cut into small pieces and taken to a "tryworks", where the actual rendering was done. Archaeologists have exposed the remains of several of these structures and found them to consist of a number of stone fireboxes, each of which supported a copper cauldron which held about 45 gallons of blubber and oil. Fires kindled with scrap wood were replenished with skin and fat from the cauldrons to fuel them during the rendering process.

The rendered and purified oil was ladled into oak and beech casks assembled by coopers who worked and lived in nearby buildings, often on terraces overlooking the tryworks. Two such structures have been excavated and have revealed the coopers' tools and personal possessions of the men who lived and worked there. The latter include ceramics, drinking glasses, knives, coins and even parts of a wooden rosary. In water-saturated areas nearby, refuse from the cooperages — barrel staves, heads and hoops, offcuts, shavings and sawdust — was found.

While the coopers enjoyed accommodation in fairly substantial buildings, many of the other crew members made do with much more humble dwellings. Many small hearths have been found, often located in small rock crevices which provided some shelter from the wind. Archaeologists believe that they are the remains of small structures that were framed with wood and covered with cloth or baleen, the plastic-like plates suspended from the whales' upper jaws which they use to strain their food from seawater.

At the extreme south end of Saddle Island, in Red Bay Harbour, the whalers' cemetery was discovered in 1982. More than 60 graves have been exposed, containing the skeletons of more than 140 individuals, With the exception of two boys aged about 12 years, all of the skeletons are those of adult European males, short of stature but of very robust build. Most are resting on their backs, heads to the west and hands folded on the chest or near the waist. The main cemetery is now restored and the original rock grave markers have been placed above the soil so that they are visible.

Some of the skeletons were remarkably well preserved while others had been almost completely dissolved by the acid groundwater. In some cases, however, the same conditions which were harmful to the bones preserved other items in the graves. In 1984, a pair of trousers and a shirt were found on an almost completely disintegrated skeleton of one of the whalers. In 1986, an individual with a large wooden cross on his chest and wearing what appears to be a cape or cloak was discovered. Speculation is that the man may have been a priest, but it is impossible to confirm this hypothesis. In the same year, in a grave some distance from the main cemetery, another set of clothes was found. This was much more complete than either of the earlier discoveries and included a knitted cap, long-sleeved shirt and jacket, knee-length trousers and stockings — all made of wool —, and a pair of leather shoes intact even to the leather ties at the front.

Archaeological work at Red Bay has continued to provide more evidence of life and work in southern Labrador during the late sixteenth century. It is the site of one of the New World's earliest industrial complexes and probably the world's first oil spill. As long as this work continues visitors are welcome at the site. They will have an opportunity to observe the excavation and preservation of the finds as well as a chance to see some of the conserved artifacts on display.